Africana Social Stratification

Africana Social Stratification

James L. Conyers Jr.

LEXINGTON BOOKS
Lanham • Boulder • New York • London

Published by Lexington Books
An imprint of The Rowman & Littlefield Publishing Group, Inc.
4501 Forbes Boulevard, Suite 200, Lanham, Maryland 20706
www.rowman.com

Unit A, Whitacre Mews, 26-34 Stannary Street, London SE11 4AB

British Library Cataloguing in Publication Information Available

The hardback edition of this book was previously catalogued by the Library of Congress
as follows:

Library of Congress Cataloging-in-Publication Data

Names: Conyers, James L., Jr., editor, author.
Title: Africana social stratification : an interdisciplinary study of
  economics, policy, and labor / edited by James L. Conyers Jr.
Description: Lanham : Lexington Books, 2017. | Includes bibliographical
  references and index.
Identifiers: LCCN 2017041238 (print) | LCCN 2017043344 (ebook) | ISBN
  9781498533157 (Electronic) | ISBN 9781498533140 (cloth : alk. paper)
Subjects: LCSH: Social stratification—United States. | Race
  discrimination—Economic aspects—United States. | African
  Americans—Economic conditions—21st century. | African Americans—Social
  conditions—21st century. | Pan-Africanism—Economic aspects.
Classification: LCC HN90.S6 (ebook) | LCC HN90.S6 A33 2017 (print) | DDC
  305.5120973—dc23
LC record available at https://lccn.loc.gov/2017041238

ISBN 978-1-4985-3314-0 (cloth : alk. paper)
ISBN 978-1-4985-3316-4 (pbk. : alk. paper)
ISBN 978-1-4985-3315-7 (electronic)

Contents

List of Figures

List of Tables

Acknowledgments

Context offers boundaries, content, and meaning for describing an issue, event, or circumstance. Located within the rubric of worldview and cultural orientation, my interpretation of reality shifts based on the levels of maturity, intuitiveness, and one's location in the season of life chances.

Captured in the vortex of empiricism at the close of the Obama administration, the issue of equity and distribution of resources is a national and popular cultural issue of dialog. The contemporary federal political climate is paused to reflect, react, and respond to international issues from a common sense perspective. Phrased another way, it becomes a daily challenge to remain in one's right mind.

Of course family is the core of the beginnings of our journeys, pursuits, and reflexive analysis. Daily, I evoke the name of my parents, James L. Conyers, Sr. and Agnes Dingle Conyers. Keeping in that tradition and custom, I evoke the name of my transitioned spouse, Jacqueline Irene Pierce-Conyers. Next up is my cub: Chad Hawkins, Sekou Conyers, and Kamau Conyers, who give me purpose and reason for the continued grind of putting in the work of research and writing. My partner Kim M. Gay, is my balance and uplift to stretch and maintain.

Bestees are always on the frontline of offering common sense and friendship for upliftment and victorious thought. Four decades of friendship breeds loyalty and respect, Qawi Jamison, Tony Robinson, Zane Corbin, James Bullock and Joe Taylor are solid Black men, fathers, and husbands, sons, who handle their business.

The entire staff of the African American Studies program at the University of Houston, are my teammates who we are ready to go daily in sharing space, information and knowledge for the sacred and secular study of Africana culture: Dr. Malachi D. Crawford, Tanja Simmons, Dormese Senegal, and

Angela Williams-Phillips. Colleagues on and off campus are also vital to my continued learning who are Professors Charnele Brown-Dozier, Pastor Alexander E.M. Johnson, Pastor Willie D. Francois, Amy Barnett DuBois, Drs. Gerald Horne, Lawrence Hogue, Billy Hawkins, Demetrius Pearson, Shayne Lee, Janis Hutchinson, George Gamble, Antonio Tillis, Tsehpo Chery, Crystal Edwards, Phillip Howard, Bruce Jones, Erika Henderson, Scot Brown, Reiland Rabaka, Abul Pitre, Christel Temple, and Kenyatta Cavil. Mentors who provide continued support are: Drs. Molefi Kete Asante, Delores P. Aldridge, Maulana Karenga, James B. Stewart, and Pastor William A. Lawson. I proceed by thanking both comrades and detractors in the process of attempting to advance research and writing in the discipline of Africana Studies.

Introduction

Africana Social Stratification is a composition of essays, which pursues from an interdisciplinary perspective, the causativeness of social inequality, impacted on African Americans. Arranged through the lens of social science research, the objective of this book endeavors to survey: sociology, economics, public policy, political science, psychology, and conceptual historical research, within the disciplinary matrix of Africana Studies. Solitarily, the query fostered, what is the short game of Africana people's quest, in their pursuit and acquisition of resources and information. Answering back I cite, what are the precedents, of prioritizing a cultural grounding of the Africana experience, which transcends social class and religious affiliation or denomination. Bamboozled about the farce of an illogical cognitive appraisal, a common-sense perspective propositions a fundamental value of up-front vindication.

Befuddling is the thought of how the Africana Studies movement of the 1980s and development of mid-level graduate and terminal degree programs, augmented and enhanced the Black middle class. One can define the Black middle class in a twofold approach. First, in the general sense of a market and economy, status is predicated on the level of wealth one has amassed, based on their net worth. Second, social division, is the level of formal education, one has attained, with emphasis on higher education. Oddly enough, African Americans can have amassed wealth and retained higher education, yet, they are still confronted with the institutionalization of racism-racialism. Based on the creation and consequences of subordinate group status, African Americans are descendants of involuntary migrants who were impacted by colonialism, annexation, and involuntary migration. Subsequently, this impact of subordination has become a fixed variable, to advance continuous systematic bigotry and inequity. Consequently, the contemporary visage of

conservatism has obstructed the headway of Affirmative Action and sup-
pressed the progression of African American prosperity.

In amity of being a social scientist, I am an ardent reader and viewer of
national newspapers and internet online interviews. After listening to the
commentary of contemporary Black public intellectuals, their prolonged
narratives, have become an appetizer—dessert, to enhance my appetite
for practical social science research entrées. Africana mis-orientation and
self-loathing has exhibited itself as a binary of narcissism—nihilism. Outcome assessments are advancing individualism or complacency of things
will never improve. Challenged in a dialectic of an either/or philosophy of
liberation, Africana people are referenced to not having the ability to make
the distinction between one's wants and needs. Phrased applicably, soon a
fool (s) will part ways with their resources and allocation of networks. The
problems which exist concerning African Americans acquisition of resources
and power is a systemic issue and not relegated to an individual enterprise of
market structuralism.

The mantra proscribed during the Reagan administration was, race was
no longer a significant issue which subordinated African Americans—in
spasm, the resolve was an issue of social class. Setting aside, what was
withdrawn from this resolution was, contextually, African Americans are
the descendants of involuntary migrants, which is built on the malice of
the creation of subordinate group status of colonialism and annexation.
Uncompromising is the idea among some African Americans, this issue of
deprivation of resources is a structural analysis, which has discern relationship or whirlwind to the methodical penalties of subsidiary assemblage
rank. Articulated another way with cynicism, if we major in the market
practical subject areas in higher education, somehow, African people will
retain a cultural collective consciousness and the concept of the Talented
Tenth will take platform.

Until now, in reviewing the basis of enslavement, one can draw attention to
the instruments of assessment, to describe and evaluate this problem of social
stratification correlated to internal and external factors. Internal, resulting
from the Africana community, not being equipped with the research analysis
of resources to study, strategize, and coordinate long and short term efforts
for resolve from their own cultural perspective and worldview. Indeed, the
cultural analysis does not answer everything, but is a beginning for Black
people to understand, their commonalities and differences from an Afrocentric worldview. External then is the basis to study and examine institutions,
and how the Eurocentric hegemonic perspective has advanced public policy,
law, and the quality of life. Contemporary national campaigns, chants, and
mantras of supremacy offer a context of ascendancy in world history and
civilization.

At the core of the research assembled is the perplexing uncertainty, who gets what and why? Phrased another way, John Henrik Clarke's assessment is referred to as, who made this arrangement? Conceiving the thought of cultural restriction, reduces Black people on the margins of having access to resources which can provide alternative outcomes in the quality of their lives. Clarke offered the apex of an Africana worldview, in his narrative and conceptual analysis of Black people visioning the world unapologetically Africana as the priority. The word-smith of the dialectic of African-centered and Afrocentric perspectives is controversial. Whereas, Clarke deposited the term Afrocentric perspective in the 1980s. However, it is Molefi Kete Asante, who takes the term into a philosophical movement of exploration. Indeed, it is the transitioned C.T. Keto, who was also a faculty member of the Temple Circle, who dropped the terminology of an African-centered perspective on History. Nonetheless, it is the preeminent Cheikh Anta Diop, who provides the pathway of the internalization of the African-centered perspective. In total, Clarke's African worldview of society, lays the basis of what is also referred as African Socialism, as the construct to provide philosophical liberation of African people globally. In this way, the issue of development, trade, and production of resources offered an alternative ontology of Black cultural development. Indeed, there several African American leadership figures who offer an industrialization method of addressing this issue of distribution of resources. Consequently, this is short lived for production, based on the flexibility of technology, international trade, and lack of formal competency in the market culture of capitalism.

Yet, in this period of the post-Obama administration, the political economy mantra is, let's make America great again. Continued in the tradition of the residual aspects of colonialism, and the back drop of the racism-racialism, the Alternative Right has emerged as the Savior, to preserve, retain and create the legacy of tradition, with emphasis on nationalism, supremacist thought of an American ethnic culture. Still, the anti-thesis of Carter G. Woodson's, *Mis-education of Negro* is ever in existence and fervent. Fundamentally, how do we make the distinction between our wants and needs. Perhaps, a simple query, but one which makes us challenge ourselves on a daily basis, to get acquisition of a meaning of self-development and cultivation. Provided in the assembly of essays, this team of scholars have attempted to raise questions, explore research, and discuss the topic of social stratification from an Afrocentric perspective. Previously, we have been offered several volumes addressing issues of resource allocation and nation building from a structural perspective. This time, the narrative and conceptual framework provides an alternative perspective and lens for assessing Black cultural autonomy from a primary basis of reference. Upholding these ideals matriculates political and cultural regression for people of African descent. In drawing upon these

Conversations, the contributors to this volume extend the parley to offer an assessment and evaluation, of the outcomes which abridge the flux of the distribution of resources predicated on priorities of the Africana experience, regulated from a Black perspective.

Chapter 1

Africana Sociology and Economics

An Interdisciplinary Analysis of Black Social Stratification

James L. Conyers Jr.

This chapter will examine the concepts of possession and ownership of Africana phenomena, with an emphasis on teaching Africana sociology and economics. Sociology is the study of group interaction, and economics is the study of the distribution and use of resources and supplies in a society. The intersection of these two fields of inquiry with an Africana perspective yields a new look at the impact of the social and economic infrastructures on involuntary migrants, with emphasis on African Americans.

Equally important, this study establishes a hypothesis to examine Africana phenomena, culture, and humanism from an Afrocentric perspective. It starts with an overview of economics, moves to a discussion of methods of analysis in assembling data and models of analysis, and concludes with a critical analysis of the topic.

OVERVIEW OF AFRICANA ECONOMICS

Economics is the study and process of producing, distributing (or exchanging), and consuming goods and services. But as with all fields of inquiry, economics does not stand alone as a discrete phenomenon. It is inevitably interwoven with other forces and structures in society. Robert Browne, for example, discusses the intimate relationship between economics and politics with relation to autonomy, especially regarding the African American community:

> The dictionary defines autonomy as "self-government"—which is essentially a political concept. Economic autonomy would presumably refer to a situation in which a group is self-supporting; that is to say, the group is not dependent upon

the largesse of others for its continued survival. Autonomy should be clearly distinguished from "autarky," a term with which it is often confused. Autarky refers to national economic self-sufficiency, whereas economic autonomy refers to the less ambitious concept of economic self-support. Black Autarky would suggest that the black community would consume only goods and services which it had itself produced. (Browne 1971)

Vernon Dixon, for his part, extends the idea of the interrelatedness of economics with his commentary on culture:

> The proposition that economics is economics and there is no black economics is consistent with a process of human learning characterized by what I call an either/or approach. People who employ this conceptual framework order their experiences in terms of polar categories or opposites. Everything falls either into this category or into that category, but not both categories at the same time. Something is either economics or not economics. Since philosophy, anthropology, psychology, sociology, et al., fall into the category of non-economics, they are considered the province of non-economists. In this context, culture, the concern of non-economics, can be considered as given rather than as determinant in economic theorizing. As a consequence, economics appears culture-free. (Dixon 1970, 425)

Likewise, Steven Erie explores the associations between policy and economics, examining the relationship between wealth and power in the public and private sectors of the United States. He addresses this issue with particular concern for the Black community:

> That the economic development of black Americans since the mid-1960s has been polarized is a now-familiar observation. This era has featured both the rise of a fledgling black middle class and the development of a near-permanent black underclass in the nation's ghettos. The economic well-being of blacks also has become, at least ostensibly, a major public policy concern during this period. Yet very little inquiry has been made into the extent to which public policy has fashioned or reinforced the polarization of black economic development. With rare exceptions, studies of the economic impacts of public policy on blacks have focused narrowly on the effects of particular government programs-affirmative action, employment, worker training, contract compliance, education, and public assistance. As a result, gauging the interrelated effects of various governmental policies has been a difficult task. (Erie 1980, 305–306)

As these scholars point out, economics is always an activity shaped by other societal influences. Keeping this in mind is the key to an analysis of social stratification. It is only when economic and sociological perspectives are brought together that we can approach issues like disparity and growth in the African American community.

METHODS OF ANALYSIS

This chapter builds upon data drawn from secondary sources to examine the interconnection between the two social science disciplines of sociology and economics. Using this "secondary analysis" approach has limitations but allows us to draw on vast resources of data about patterns of disparity exhibited toward the distribution of support and resources of Africana phenomena on an international level. The data sources are focused specifically on African Americans, Black economics, and social stratification. And a particular emphasis on context provides a check on easy conclusions. For example, Richard Schaefer discusses how the sociological context provides a more illuminating view of purely economic data, as he analyzes trends in African American income:

> Much of the apparent gain in African American incomes is misleading, for it may not signify a better life, as is usually assumed. First, Black family income is more likely to depend upon two sources of income, with both husband and wife working. Second, Blacks have consistently migrated to areas with higher living costs, say from farms to cities, where increased income barely keeps pace with the increased costs. Third, Blacks are especially hard hit at times of increased unemployment. (Schaefer 1993)

Context becomes the operative term in reference to locating the subject matter in space, and time. Culture is the key to the description and evaluation of Africana sociology and economics, using an Afrocentric interpretive analysis of *Ujamaa* (the Kiswahili term for cooperative economics). Figure 1.1 charts the flow of culture from a survey perspective in four points:

1. History: A record of human events in the image and interests of the narrator.
2. Mythology: A version of historical treatment, based on season in life, with relation to space, place, and time.
3. Motif: Signs and symbols, which reaffirm a people in their own image and interest.
4. Ethos: Reflection of accountability and memory of a people, from one generation to another.

Relative to this analysis of culture, Pan-Africanism has a twofold approach to explaining and assessing Africana phenomena: global and continental. The global perspective refers to the unification of African people throughout the world, whereas the continental perspective refers to the unification of African people throughout the continent of Africa. When we analyze the access to materials, goods, or services, in the space of private or public sector, both the

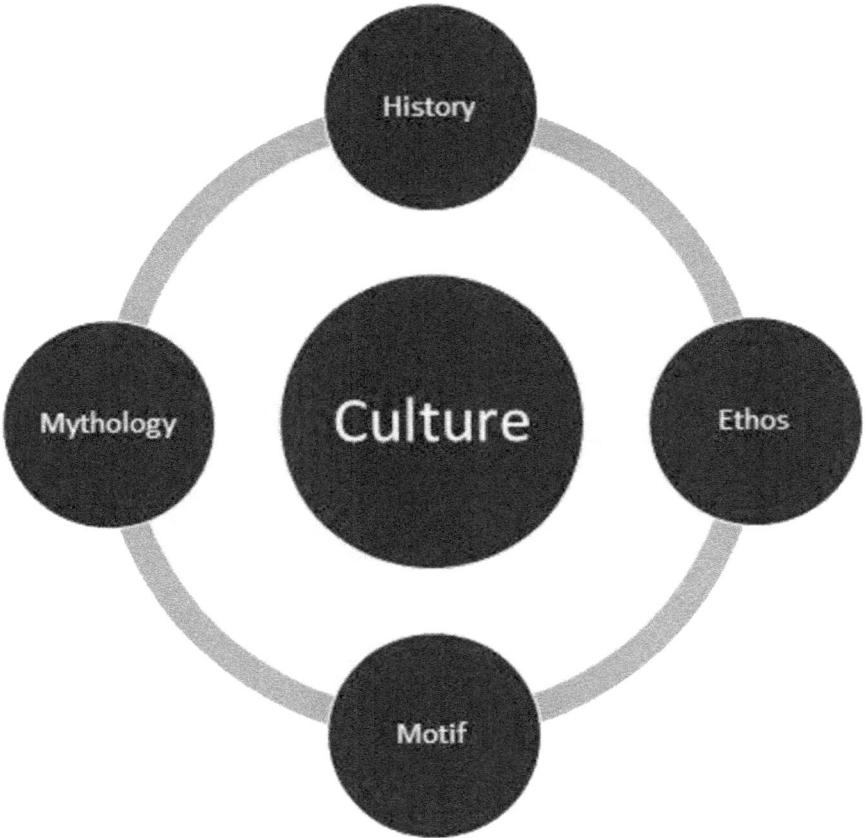

Figure 1.1   The Flow of Culture in Four Critical Points.

global and continental approaches come into play. They bring to the discussion of African American economics a perspective grounded in the process of regulating the access to economic goods and the possibility of any group of people having sovereignty over their economic life.

ECONOMIC IMPACT OF RACE AND CLASS

Economic analysis in the United States is the study of transfer of goods and services within a market structure. That market structure, however, has two components: the regular economy and the irregular economy. The irregular economy consists of the transfer of services and goods that are not reported to the federal and state governments and that consequently are not taxed or folded into the computations of data from the regular economy.

In studying American economics in general, it is also critical to distinguish between the influences of class and of race. As Maulana Karenga writes, "First, both race and class are the bases of black exploitation and oppression. . . . In fact, the interpretation of the source of solution to Black oppression can in fact end up as a class focused interpretation rather than an overall Black one" (Karenga, 343). Talmadge Anderson discusses the specifically racial component of American economics and how that impacts efforts toward Black economic liberation:

> The economic system of America is not exalt and immune from criticism by black people. Moreover, the exploitive nature and intent of American capitalism by its racial subjugation of black people, naturally, should provoke the most vociferous attack on the system by black economists and academicians. This is not to say that white society or the dominant culture, in the absence of humanistic values, should not laud and defend American economic practices. It would be insensible, barring morality, for white beneficiaries to decry the pseudo-democratic system that has afforded them the apex of human vantage and affluence. Likewise, it is equally illogical and perhaps even unnatural for black people to cherish a socio-economic system or institution which demeans and exploits, so blatantly, on the basis of black color. (Anderson 1970, 11)

The tendency in economic discourse, influenced by the neoconservative mindset, has been to emphasize class status and dismiss the idea that race continues to affect the economic progress of African Americans. This is all the more reason that a sociological perspective must accompany any study of economics and avoid the most simplistic conclusions or assertions.

Sociological Impact of Race and Class

One of the most pressing questions in Black sociology is the significance of race and class in Black life. The significance of the question rests not only in its relevance to understanding Black oppression but also in its relevance to generating strategies for development and liberation. Ronald Mincy draws attention to this issue in the wake of Equal Employment Opportunity Commission regulations regarding hiring and promotion:

> Several studies have suggested that civil rights legislation and enforcement reduced Black-White earnings disparities. For example, Freeman found that EEOC expenditures per non-White worker significantly increased the relative income of Black workers. Also, Farley reported declining Black-White disparities in the rates of return on investments in education, training, and migration.

While this is strong evidence that discrimination has declined, Blacks continue to earn less than similarly qualified Whites.

Some observers have expressed concern that affirmative action in hiring increased the disparities within the Black community. By giving employers incentives to hire and promote those Blacks with the most work experience or education, because these actions would be easiest to justify, employers may have hired Blacks for upper-level positions and avoided hiring them for lower-level positions. (Mincy 1989, 262)

Being fully aware of these sociological impacts requires the type of Afrocentric awareness that Asante (2003) posited. Asante's levels of transformation (Figure 1.2) shows the multiple elements that will affect African American identity and any attempt to describe and evaluate social stratification.

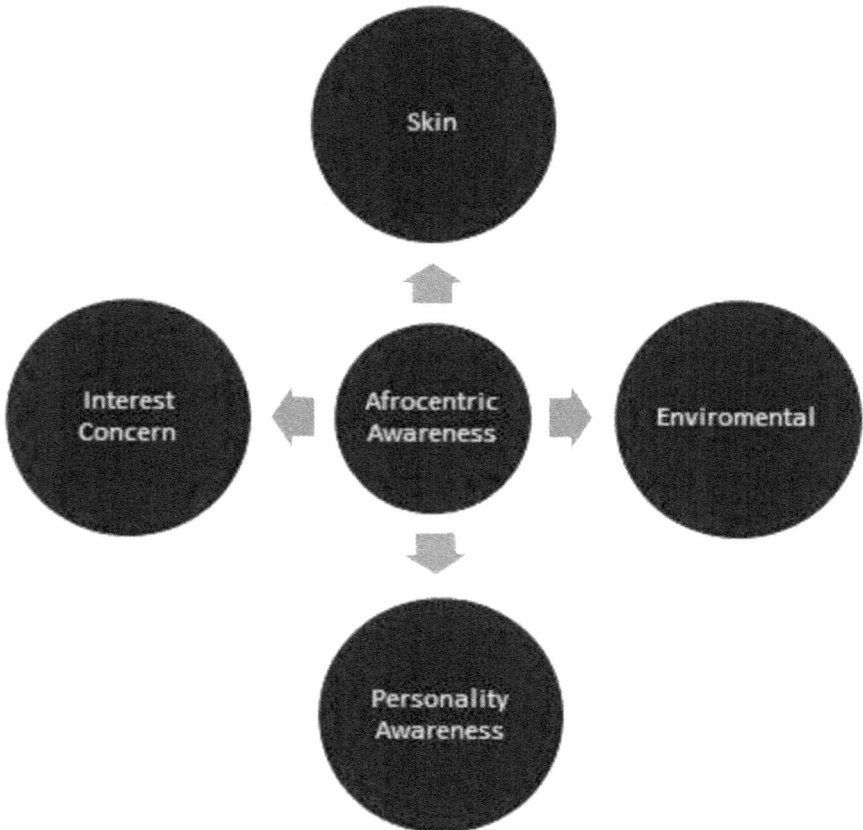

Figure 1.2   Afrocentric Awareness (adapted from Asante 2003).

The Class Question

The focus on class as the fundamental unit of social analysis and the key determinant in social life has been provided most definitively by the sociology of Marxism. Marx argued essentially that the shape and functioning of society was determined by its economic foundation and that class, as a socio-economic category, was basic to the understanding of society and history.

Despite the Marxist emphasis on class as the great determining factor, Blauner (1972:31) also calls attention to the fact that often in a racist society, racial exploitation and/or control becomes "an end itself, despite its original limited purpose as a means to exploitation and privilege." Thus, the factor of "covert or institutional racism has a dynamic of its own, despite the vagaries of prejudice and bigotry, real as they are." Moreover, recent literature argues the persistence of race as a major determinant in life chances and life conditions.

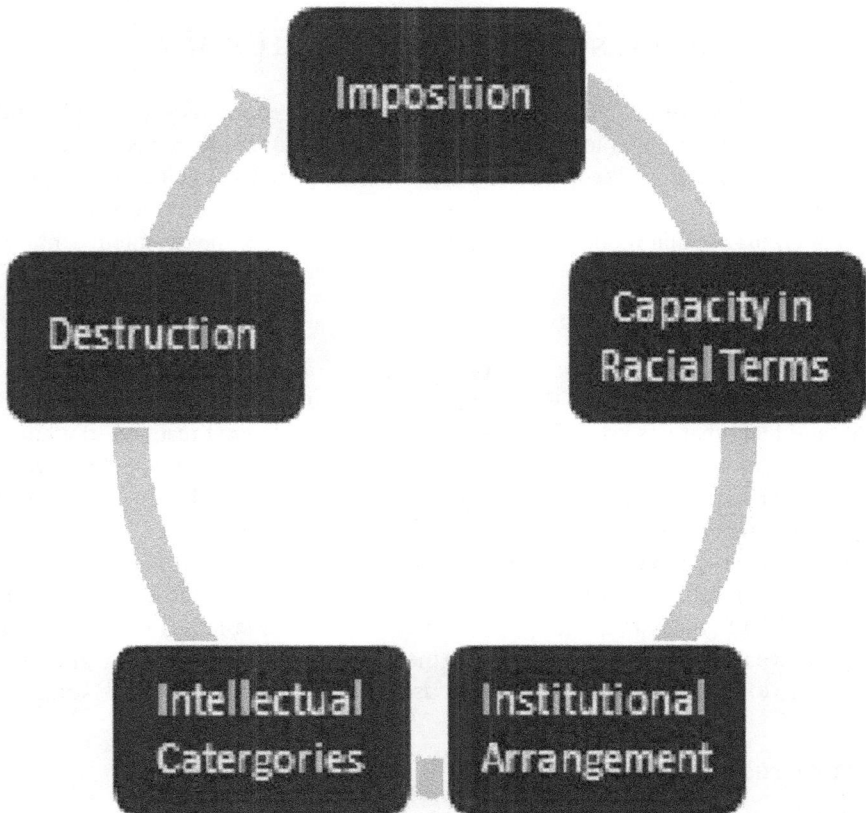

Figure 1.3   Social Structures.

Racism begins with the creation and mystification of race. It is a type of social thought and practice that expresses itself in three basic ways:

1. The imposition (i.e., conquest and oppression of a people) and interruption, destruction, and appropriation of a people's history and productive capacity in racial terms.
2. An ideology (i.e., an elaborate system of pseudo-intellectual categories, assumptions, and contentions) negative to peoples of color and serving as justification of the imposition and reinforcement of the institutional arrangement.
3. An institutional arrangement (i.e., a system of political, economic, and social structures) that ensures white power and privilege over peoples of color.

Figure 1.3 offers a structural analysis of these core components of racism.

MODELS OF ECONOMIC DEVELOPMENT

Because of the tight relationship between culture and economics in real life, and the importance of sociology to economics as an area of study, ideas of race permeate the economic development models that have been developed to explain African American economic progress or obstacles. This section looks at some of the most popular models of race theory in the course of the twentieth century.

The Deficiency Paradigm

Social scientists of varying ideological orientation (i.e., conservative, liberal, Marxist) have argued that Blacks have no real culture, that slavery destroyed it, and that what passed as Black was simply a pathological reaction to whites, a duplication of them or an expression of lower-class culture rather than a specific Black culture. Myrdal (1944, 927–930) argued that the Black person is "an exaggerated American" and essentially a "pathological" reaction to whites.

This paradigm has been largely discredited. The Black cultural revolution of the 1960s reaffirmed not only the beauty and integrity of Black culture, continental and Diasporan, and its difference from white culture in terms of life goals, worldview, and values, but also the need to draw on its African and mass sources to recreate it, revitalize it, and use it as a weapon in the Black struggle.

The Crusian Paradigm

Harold Cruse (1967) in his massive study of culture and politics in Harlem, *The Crisis of the Negro Intellectual,* made a profound contribution to the

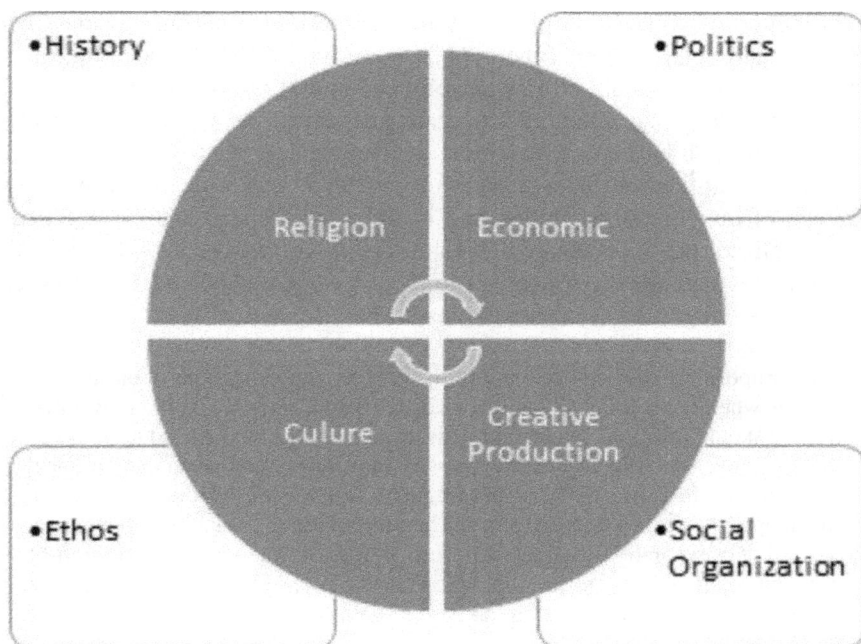

Figure 1.4 The Kawaida Paradigm.

focus on cultural revitalization and struggle. The role of the Black intellectual begins with recognition of the cultural base of power in this country as expressed in the power of European ethnic groups.

The Kawaida Paradigm

Maulana Karenga (1967, 1980, 1997, 2002) contends that the key challenge in Black life is the cultural crisis and that Africans must recover the best of their culture and use it to envision a new world and to support the struggle to bring that world into being. Figure 1.4 provides a snapshot of the components and dynamics of Black community life.

CONCLUSION

This chapter has explored the intersection of sociology and economics in the study of African American progress. In the classroom, its implication is that we must pay careful attention to context when teaching about African American economics and the problems of disparity. Social stratification—the distribution of goods and opportunities—is determined not just by class but by race and being aware of the models of African American sociology will help educators be aware of how sociological modes of thought influence our ideas about who has made the economic rules about poverty and the continued subordination of Black economic development.

Social stratification focuses on who gets what and why. Because of the impact of involuntary migration and institutional racism, Blacks have been marginalized and subordinated to attain equity of resources. Awareness of these forces will allow our analysis to more clearly see the end point to such debates as integration or separation, as Lerone Bennett writes:

> The proposition is liberation by any means necessary. And the point at issue here is whether the proposition, as clarified, depends on the question of whether blacks should integrate or separate. This question, which has stirred up so much controversy, which has launched so many movements and generated so much rhetoric and heat and light, is meaningless on the level of policy, as a close reading of the proposition will show. The proposition says that the fundamental issue is not separation or integration but liberation. The either/or question of integration or separation does not speak to that proposition: for if our goal is liberation it may be necessary to do both or neither. (Bennett 1972)

American economic life has been grounded on the systemic subordination of a selected group of people. Possibly, we can develop alternate methods and approaches, using an interdisciplinary approach, to substantiate equity, fairness, and outcome measures for the advancement of African American social stratification.

BIBLIOGRAPHY

Anderson, Talmadge. 1970. "Black Economic Liberation under Capitalism." *The Black Scholar* 2(2):11–14.

Asante, Molefi Kete. 2003. *Afrocentricity: The Theory of Social Change.* Chicago: African American Images.

Bennett, Lerone, Jr. 1972. *The Challenge of Blackness.* Chicago: Johnson Publishing Company.

Blauner, Robert. 1972. *Racial Oppression in America.* New York: Harper and Row, Publishers.

Browne, Robert S. 1971. "Black Economic Autonomy." *The Black Scholar* 3(2), Black Economics (October): 26–31.

Cruse, Harold. 1967. *The Crisis of the Negro Intellectual: A Historical Analysis of the Failure of Black Leadership.* New York: Morrow.

Dixon, Vernon J. 1970. "The Di-unital Approach to 'Black Economics'." *The American Economic Review* 60(2), Papers and Proceedings of the Eighty-Second Annual Meeting of the American Economic Association (May): 424–429, 425.

Erie, Steven P. 1980. "Public Policy and Black Economic Polarization." *Policy Analysis* 6(3): 305–317, 305–306.

Maulana Karenga. 2010. *Introduction to Black Studies.* Los Angeles, CA: University of Sankore Press.

Mincy, Ronald B. 1989. "Paradoxes in Black Economic Progress: Incomes, Families, and the Underclass." *The Journal of Negro Education* 58(3), Shaping the Urban Future: People and Places, Problems and Potentials (Summer): 255–262, 262.

Mydral, Gunnar. 1944. *An American Dilemma.* New York: Harper and Row Publishers.

Schaefer, Richard T. 1993. *Racial and Ethnic Groups.* New York: Harper College Publishers, 224.

Chapter 2

The Emerging Field of Stratification Economics

A Unified Social Science Theory of Race and Inequality?

Gregory Price

Since its founding and genesis in the eighteenth century, economics and political economy struggled with the idea that the scope of it social science presumed behavioral homogeneity among humans (Peart and Levy 2004). This was assumed to be particularly true with respect to nonwhites, for whom it was often posited and simply not equipped—for genetic and/or cultural reasons—with the behavioral or cultural apparatus to thrive and prosper in a market-oriented society (Darity 1994). Such presumptions dominated the theoretical and empirical methodology of economics up through contemporary times, rationalizing the causes and consequences of black-white economic inequality to be attributable to the unobserved behavioral characteristics of blacks that results in their inferior equilibrium outcomes relative to whites.

The rejection of the "human homogeneity postulate" (Peart and Levy 2004) as it applies to blacks has at least two significant consequences. First, it conditions an influential research methodology that determines academic careers and public policy. Black economists who reject black behavioral heterogeneity as a driver of black-white inequality face barriers in getting published in economics journals (Mason, Myers, and Darity 2005), which can constrain their prospects for success in an academy that has been historically hostile to their presence (Price 2009). Second, it disproportionately influences public policy as it constitutes a high-profile research methodology embraced and marketed by institutions such as the National Bureau of Economic Research—a prepublication outlet for economists at our nation's top research universities that embraces unobserved behavioral/cultural heterogeneity among the black and disadvantaged as a methodological virtue and as a prerequisite for designing public policy to ameliorate black-white economic inequality.

The appeal to behavioral and/or cultural heterogeneity among the black and disadvantaged as an explanation for black-white inequality ultimately anchors black disadvantage in a narrative of behavioral and cultural dysfunction. This narrative bolsters research and policy agendas that presume a genetic/cultural inferiority of blacks and so assert that inequality is not amenable to activist policy interventions that require a redistribution of opportunity and resources (Darity 2005). Darity examines this narrative and proposes *stratification economics* as a more productive theory of race and inequality. In this chapter, I extend Darity's proposition and advance the human homogeneity postulate as a sensible and uncontroversial axiom, consistent with the parsimony principles for engaging science that should inform social science research methodology. In addition, similar to Markus (2008), I posit that any observed race-specific behaviors are not exogenous—determined by race—but endogenous, constituting responses expected universally of all optimizing agents—the workhorse analytical device of modern economics.

THE HUMAN HOMOGENEITY POSTULATE AS PRINCIPLE OF SOUND SOCIAL SCIENCE

The Austrian physicist and philosopher of science Ernst Mach concluded that "Science itself, therefore, may be regarded as a minimal problem, consisting of the completest possible presentment of facts with the *least possible expenditure of thought*" (Mach 1893, 490). This Machian principle is a case for parsimony in scientific method, which, as maintained by Gabaix and Laibson (2008), provides several benefits for economics research. First, parsimonious theories and models in economics are ideal as they prevent the researcher from consciously or subconsciously manipulating the model so that it overfits the available facts and data. Second, adding additional parameters to a model increases complexity, rendering it easy to explain in-sample data at the expense of generalizing a particular class of phenomena outside of the sample.

Appealing to unobserved behavioral heterogeneity when considering black-white differences in economic outcomes does indeed add additional parameters to economic theory and its associated empirics. As a research strategy, by departing from the assumption of human behavioral homogeneity, appealing to unobserved behavioral heterogeneity also undermines the scope of optimization by agents by implicitly assuming that some agents, like blacks, either can't optimize or optimize poorly, reminiscent of Irving Fisher's (1930) racial theory of time preference in which some racial groups were simply too impatient to postpone current consumption. Given the Machian principle, if economic science aspires to be a sound social science, appealing to unobserved behavioral heterogeneity at the expense of the assumption of human behavioral homogeneity undermines the principle of parsimony.

Invoking and maintaining human behavioral homogeneity as a social science principle also coheres with the principle of Occam's Razor, a heuristic for science methodology that is a precursor to the Machian principle. Kelly and Mayo-Wilson (2010) formally prove that scientists who systematically favor simpler theories minimize errors and the number and timeliness of retractions of opinion. This suggests that simple models enable the shortest path to the true scientific theory governing a particular phenomenon. The empirical virtue of simple minimal assumption models are also attractive, as Kelly (2007) finds that they possibly enable more efficient statistical inference—a significant component of causal inference in economics in particular and the social sciences in general. In this context, a minimal assumption of human behavioral homogeneity enables efficient identification of the causal effects of race on a wide variety of outcomes of interest to social scientists. Thus, to the extent that anthropologist, economists, and sociologists aspire to provide a causal account of race, an analytical framework that assumes human behavioral homogeneity becomes a candidate framework for a unified social science theory of race and inequality, as it constitutes a parsimonious and efficient methodological approach to discovering the true causes and consequences of race.

STRATIFICATION ECONOMICS AS A PARSIMONIOUS AND UNIFIED SOCIAL SCIENCE

Darity (2005) proposes stratification economics as a robust alternative to the conventional social science methodological and theoretical approach to race and inequality. Stratification economics constitutes a theoretical and empirical framework that considers the rational and material basis for group and identity formation, both for membership in dominant and subordinate groups. Similar to anthropology, sociology, and in some instances political science, stratification economics views the group as an important and perhaps fundamental unit of analysis. A primary aim of stratification economics is identifying the causal effects of group and identity, its existence and formation, on a wide variety of disparities (e.g., income, health, wealth, unemployment). A major axiom of stratification economics is that in all ascriptively identifiable social groups (e.g., race, ethnicity) there will be some individuals who engage in self-defeating or dysfunctional behavior, but such behavior is not collectively shared or characteristic of the group (Darity 2005). It is this axiom that, along Machian scientific methodology principles, renders stratification economics a robust theory of race and inequality.

In general, ruling out self-defeating and dysfunctional behavior as a general behavioral characteristic reduces the complexity of models that aim to discover the truth about racial inequality by providing a shorter path to the truth about the governing mechanisms that explain racial inequality in a wide variety of outcomes of interest to anthropologists, economists, sociologists, and so on. In particular, stratification economics does not require increasing the complexity, and reducing the simplicity of, social science theories of race and inequality by introducing the notion of unobserved behavioral heterogeneity, as it takes seriously the human homogeneity postulate. This reduction of complexity helps realize Machian standards for science—in this instance social science—enabling a parsimonious and efficient method to identify the causes and consequences of race and inequality.

For a stratification economist, race serves as a primitive argument in the mechanisms (e.g., utility or profit function) determining choice in social and market interactions and their subsequent outcomes. As such, the core input into rational decisions by optimizing agents in their person-to-person interactions is membership in a race-group—actual or perceived. Theoretically, one can rationalize why race is a primitive argument in the preference functions of dominant racial groups by an appeal to Glenn Loury's theory of racial stigma (Loury 2002), whereby the dominant racial group's perception of blacks as inferior engender a persistent cycle of self-fulfilling prophesies that endogenizes black disadvantage and reinforces notions of black inferiority, which in turn justifies the persistent maltreatment of blacks in social and market interactions. In this context, race is a primitive argument in the preference functions of dominant racial groups and explains the outcomes of subordinate racial groups. To the extent that blackness or nonwhiteness as a stigma results in outcome disparities for subordinate racial groups, it can also rationally induce some—without an appeal to behavioral or cultural heterogeneity—to optimally invest in an identity (Fang and Loury 2005) that is abhorred and ridiculed by mainstream society, resulting in further marginalization and subordination.

It is also instructive to point out another methodological virtue of stratification economics—the importance of relative racial group position as a driver of racial inequality. Allowing race or "whiteness" to be a primitive argument of preference functions operationalizes, without a need to reduce the simplicity and parsimony of models, the material benefits associated with group identity and the dominant racial group's attitudes toward and treatment of the subordinate group. As a marker of group membership, stratification economics permits an explanation of why race matters in a decision-theoretical manner, as being a member of the dominant racial group, or being measurably close enough, has tangible material benefits that engender disparities. Indeed there is evidence that "whiteness" as measured by perceived skin tone or even verbal traits (like "sounding black" or "sounding white") (Grogger 2011) can explain disparities in an array of scenarios, from criminal sentencing (Gyimah-Brempong and Price 2006) to marriage (Hamilton, Goldsmith and Darity 2009) to labor market outcomes (Goldsmith, Hamilton, and Darity 2007).

Stratification economics rationalizes the persistence of racial discrimination and inequality by highlighting the payoffs of being part of a dominant racial group. As such, it improves upon the standard neoclassical economics appeal to discriminatory tastes that can only persist due to noncompetitive market structures (Becker 1957) and information deficits/asymmetries (Phelps 1972). As there are clear tangible returns to being a dominant racial group, and such groups have incentives to maintain their relative position, stratification economics can explain a wide variety of dominant group power dynamics and inequalities that are of interest to anthropology, sociology, political science, and the interdisciplinary social sciences (e.g., public health, ethnic/black studies, public policy). It is in this last context that is perhaps the more obvious case for stratification economics being a unified social science theory of race and inequality. Its parsimonious specification of how race matters and the attendant tangible payoffs to being a dominant racial group can explain and rationalize a wide variety of, perhaps all, observed race-based disparities.

CONCLUSION

This chapter has proposed that the emerging field of stratification economics is potentially a unified social science theory of race and inequality. A consideration of the method and scope of stratification economics reveals that by embracing the human homogeneity postulate, it provides a parsimonious social scientific framework for explaining a wide variety of race-based disparities. Given the Machian principle for science, stratification economics explains a maximum amount of race-based disparities with minimum model complexity.

Of course, there is no consensus in science on parsimony having supreme epistemic virtue (Baker 2007; Cowling 2013). However, as Cowling (2013) suggests, a case for ideological parsimony can also be made as a criterion for science—the range of primitive notions about the structure of reality embedded in a theory. In this sense, stratification economics poses minimum structure on presumptions about the laws of reality. It does not commit itself to an restrictive ideology about the laws of reality, by assuming, for example, that markets are efficient or that they promote optimal human welfare. Stratification economics only presumes that race is a primitive argument that determines preferences and outcomes. And it recognizes that ideology itself can emerge as a strategy by dominant racial groups to preserve their relative power over subordinate racial groups (Fields 1982, 1990).

BIBLIOGRAPHY

Baker, Alan. 2007. "Occam's Razor in Science: A Case Study from Biogeography." *Biology and Philosophy* 22(2): 193–215.

Becker, Gary S. 1957. *The Economics of Discrimination*. Chicago: University of Chicago Press.

Cowling, Sam. 2013. "Ideological Parsimony." *Synthese* 190(17): 3889–3908.

Darity, William. 1994. "Many Roads to Extinction: Early AEA American Economic Association Economists and the Black Disappearance Hypothesis." *History of Economics Review* 21 (Winter): 47–64.

———. 2005. "Stratification Economics: The Role of Intergroup Inequality." *Journal of Economics and Finance* 29(2): 144–53.

Fang, Hanming, and Glenn C. Loury. 2005. "Dysfunctional Identities Can Be Rational." *American Economic Review* 95(2): 104–11.

Fields, Barbara Jeanne. 1982. "Ideology and Race in American History." In *Region, Race, and Reconstruction: Essays in Honor of C. Vann Woodward*, edited by J. Morgan Kousser and James M. McPherson, 143–77. New York: Oxford University Press.

———. 1990. "Slavery, Race and Ideology in the United States of America." *New Left Review* 181: 95–118.

Fisher, Irving. 1930. *The Theory of Interest, as Determined by Impatience to Spend Income and Opportunity to Invest It*. New York: Macmillan.

Gabaix, Xavier, and David Laibson. 2008. "The Seven Properties of Good Models." In *The Foundations of Positive and Normative Economics: A Handbook*, edited by Andrew Caplin and Andrew Schotter, 292–299. Oxford: Oxford University Press.

Goldsmith, Arthur H., Darrick Hamilton, and William Darity Jr. 2007. "From Dark to Light: Skin Color and Wages Among African Americans." *Journal of Human Resources* 42(4): 701–738.

Grogger, Jeffrey. 2011. "Speech Patterns and Racial Wage Inequality." *Journal of Human Resources* 46(1): 1–25.

Gyimah-Brempong, Kwabena, and Gregory Price. 2006. "Crime and Punishment and Skin Hue Too?" *American Economic Review* 96(2): 246–250.

Hamilton, Darrick, Arthur H. Goldsmith, and William Darity Jr. 2009. "Shedding Light on Marriage: The Influence of Skin Shade on Marriage for Black Females." *Journal of Economic Behavior and Organization* 72(1): 30–56.

Kelly, Kevin T. 2007. "Ockham's Razor, Empirical Complexity, and Truth-Finding Complexity." *Theoretical Computer Science* 382(2–3): 270–289.

Kelly, Kevin T., and Conor Mayo-Wilson. 2010. "Ockham Efficiency Theorem for Stochastic Empirical Methods." *Journal of Philosophical Logic* 39(6): 679–712.

Loury, Glenn C. 2002. *The Anatomy of Racial Inequality*. Cambridge, MA: Harvard University Press.

Mach, Ernst. 1893. *The Science of Mechanics: A Critical and Historical Exposition of Its Principles*. Chicago: Open Court.

Markus, Hazel Rose. 2008. "Pride, Prejudice, and Ambivalence: Toward a Unified Theory of Race and Ethnicity." *American Psychologist* 63(8): 651–670.

Mason, Patrick L., Samuel L. Myers, and William A. Darity. 2005. "Is There Racism in Economic Research?" *European Journal of Political Economy* 21(3): 755–761.

Peart, Sandra J., and David M. Levy. 2004. "The Negro Science of Exchange: Classical Economics and Its Chicago Revival." In *Race, Liberalism, and Economics*, edited by David C. Colander, Robert E. Prasch, and Falguni A. Sheth, 56–84. Ann Arbor: University of Michigan Press.

Phelps, Edmund S. 1972. "The Statistical Theory of Racism and Sexism." *American Economic Review* 62(4): 659–661.

Price, Gregory N. 2009. "The Problem of the 21st Century: Economics Faculty and the Color Line." *Journal of Socio-Economics* 38(2): 331–343.

Chapter 3

Frontstage and Backstage Racial Performances

The Contributions of Backstage Methodological Research

Brittany Slatton

Donald Sterling, onetime owner of the NBA's Los Angeles Clippers, did not intend for his attitudes toward blacks to become public, "frontstage" knowledge. These were attitudes expressed during a private "backstage" conversation with the then girlfriend V. Stiviano. However, when Stiviano made a secret tape of the conversation available to the press, Sterling quickly found himself embroiled in controversy and was tasked with trying to explain his racial attitudes to the public.

This was not Donald Sterling's first time being accused of racism. Former employee and NBA player Elgin Baylor unsuccessfully sued him for discrimination. And in 2006, Sterling was successfully sued by the Justice Department for racially discriminating against blacks and Latinos who sought residence in several apartment buildings he owned (Glover 2009). However, it was Sterling's backstage racial expressions—brought to the forefront by a former girlfriend—that ultimately led to his downfall.

Sterling, like other whites like Paula Deen who found themselves in similar situations, claimed that he was not a racist. He justified this by citing his number of black "friends" and his NAACP lifetime achievement award from the Los Angeles chapter. Despite Sterling's claim of innocence, the players' association of the NBA—a league comprised of over 70 percent black players—along with community members, demanded the removal of Sterling from his position as team owner. These demands led Adam Silver—the NBA commissioner—to administer a lifetime ban against Sterling and force the sale of his team.

Over the past decades, many intellectuals have argued that post–civil rights society has moved into a new racial regime (Bonilla-Silva 2011), whereby old-fashioned expressions of racism—rooted in black biological inferiority and segregation—have been replaced by a *new racism*, one that is more subtle and covert. A bevy of scholars developed several new racism theories to best explain the contemporary ways in which white racism operates in modern society. Many such scholars have debated the relevancy of one new racial theory over the other. In this chapter, I question whether whites have indeed replaced old-fashioned, segregationist racism at all. As in the case of Donald Sterling, it may be that whites still regularly express old-fashioned racist attitudes in private.

To address this research inquiry, this chapter considers the usefulness of the backstage methodological approach for both accessing and analyzing white racism in contemporary society. First, I discuss the theories of a "new racism" and the argument against it. Second, I provide a detailed introduction to the backstage methodological approach, including the conceptualization of backstage studies, the major approaches, findings, and contributions to the field. Lastly, I consider potential criticisms and limitations of backstage studies and the broader implications of backstage research on racism.

A NEW RACISM?

The achievement of de jure equality in the 1970s culminated in the banning of "segregated schools," prohibition of "discrimination in employment and public accommodations," and the passing "of anti-discrimination law and affirmative action" policies (Pager 2007, 106). De jure equality also brought about several social changes. Society endorsed "the principles of racial equality," strategically adopted color-blind ideology (and later post-racial ideology), repudiated racism and discrimination, and sanctioned individuals who engaged blatant, overt acts of racism (National Research Council 2004). Traditional polls and surveys now show a "decline in overt or Jim Crow–style prejudice among whites" (Bonilla-Silva 2011). Whites perform well on racial distance scales, appear committed to the principles of equal treatment, adopt color-blind ideals, and do not consider themselves racist; indeed many define themselves as anti-racist (Schuman et al. 2001; Devine and Elliot 1995; Jones 2005, 2011; DiTomaso 2013).

Despite these seemingly progressive white racial attitudes, myriad sociological and psychological studies find consistent evidence of racial bias against blacks in labor and lending markets and the criminal justice system (Bertrand and Mullainathan 2004; Pager and Quillian 2005; Pager 2003; Massey and Denton 1993; Center for Constitutional Rights 2012; New York Civil Liberties Union 2013; American Civil Liberties Union 2013). Furthermore, research on white behaviors reveal that a substantial portion of whites avoid interacting with blacks (and other people of color); are uncomfortable in interracial situations; avoid predominantly black neighborhoods, schools, and churches; exclude black women and men as online dating options; and are least likely to marry blacks in comparison to other ethnicities or racial groups of color (Emerson and Smith 2000; Trawalter and Richeson 2008; Richeson and Trawalter 2005; Shelton 2003; Mendes et al. 2002; Robnett and Feliciano 2011; Feliciano, Robnett, and Komaie 2009; U.S. Census Bureau 2010; Lin and Lundquist 2013; Qian and Lichter 2007; Yancey 2007).

The contradiction between persistent racial discrimination in a society that has achieved de jure equality and that boasts of its racially progressive, color-blind ideology has led some intellectuals to argue that we have entered a new racial regime (Leach 2005). According to these intellectuals, old-fashioned racism—rooted in black biological inferiority and segregation—has been replaced with new, subtle, symbolic, and/or covert racism that allows whites to buttress the existing racial order by focusing on cultural deficiencies and denying racial discrimination—all while claiming or appearing to be nonracist (Bonilla-Silva 2011).

Several theories characterize this new formal expression of racism. According to Kinder and Sears (1981) society reflects a symbolic racism that is defined as a "negative affect directed at blacks" based on a belief that "racial discrimination is no longer a serious obstacle to blacks' prospects for a good life" and that blacks are disadvantaged because they do not adopt "American values" (Henry and Sears 2002, 254; Kinder and Sears 1981; Tarman and Sears 2005). According to Bobo, Kluegel, and Smith (1997) society reflects laissez faire racism, which entails the persistence of black racial stereotypes and white resistance to programs designed to end racism. Dovidio and Gaertner (2001, 2004) find evidence of an aversive racism, whereby whites express "contemporary racial bias ... in indirect ways" that do not threaten a "non-prejudiced self-image." While Bonilla-Silva (2011, 191) finds that contemporary society is characterized by a new racism that is "subtle" and anchored by a color-blind racism that "rationalizes the status of minorities as the product of market dynamics, naturally occurring phenomena, and their alleged cultural deficiencies."

Picca and Feagin (2007, 22), however, argue that "one must be careful ... in reaching conclusions about a 'new racism' or a 'colorblind racism' that is greatly different from the past." They argue that new and subtle forms of racism that focus on cultural differences as opposed to biological ones are not new (Leach 2005; Picca and Feagin 2007). Research shows that the "expression of racial inferiority" *and* "the denial of societal discrimination (or a criticism of cultural difference)" were both popular ideologies before the achievement of de jure equality (Leach 2005, 441). Whites did not especially rely on old-fashioned racism in the pre–civil rights era, and this expression of racism was not as overt and blatant as some might assume. Leach (2005, 435) finds that an analysis of qualitative and quantitive studies on formal expressions of segregationism from the 1940s to the 1960s reveals that "even where segregation was a popular practice, there was great variation" in the expression of old-fashioned, segregationist racism. While segregationist racism was certainly more popular during the era of de jure inequality, studies show that only half of whites were actually "willing to make a formal expression of 'old-fashioned' segregationism" during that time (Leach 2005, 435). Similarly, historical data shows that "formal expressions of cultural differences" and the "denial of societal discrimination" are "long-standing features of societies that espouse democratic egalitarianism" (Leach 2005, 434). For example, in 1946, more than 60 percent of whites believed blacks received fair treatment in society. Thus, the ideological underpinnings of a proposed new racism are not unique to the post–civil rights society but have in fact been an integral part of society for a long time now (Leach 2005).

Hence, what explains the continued existence of racial inequality in a society that is supposedly racially progressive? Perhaps researchers need to employ different methodological approaches that better access the machinations of racism in contemporary society. In the following sections of this chapter, I address this question by considering the usefulness of backstage methodological approaches, which employ strategic methods to analyze white attitudes, behaviors, and emotions in inconspicuous white spaces: the backstage.

THE METHODOLOGY OF BACKSTAGE STUDIES

Backstage studies offer new methodological approaches for the analysis of white racism by accessing the behaviors, emotions, and attitudes of whites in private, comfortable spaces—where they are less likely to be influenced by social desirability bias (when respondents provide responses that are socially acceptable and normative in society). Backstage research on racial attitudes and behaviors is still relatively new in the social sciences and only a small body of work actually examines whites in the backstage (Eliasoph 1999; Myers and Williamson 2001; McKinney 2005; Picca and Feagin 2007; Myers 2005; Hughey 2001; Slatton 2014; Embrick and Henricks 2015).

The backstage approach is primarily conceptualized from sociologist Erving Goffman's dramaturgical model of social interaction. Goffman used the theatrical stage as a metaphor for human performances (Goffman 1959). He contended that people are social actors who engage in performances—employing props, jargon, and other social tools—to impress upon others (their audience) a preferred social identity (Jacobsen and Kristiansen 2015). Different situations come with different audiences and settings; hence social actors must constantly adapt "the self-images presented in [their] everyday-life performances ... to changing social situations" (Jacobsen and Kristiansen 2015). Goffman (1959) identifies two main regions or sociospatial settings that social actors perform in: the front region (here referred to as the frontstage) and the back region (the backstage). The frontstage is the region where social actors are concerned with projecting an "appropriate" self-image that accords with the normative expectations of society (Goffman 1959; Smith 2008, 220; Jacobsen and Kristansen 2015). The backstage is where the "performer can relax; he can drop his front, forgo speaking his lines, and step out of character" (Goffman 1959, 115). Goffman (1959, 123) referred to the transition between the frontage and backstage as "a wonderful putting on and taking off character."

Following this dramaturgical metaphor, backstage research studies are concerned with the types of *racial performances* that whites *do* in a given social situation and the ways in which their performances communicate particular social identities concerning their racial beliefs, attitudes, behaviors, and emotions. Hence, researchers examine the different types of racial performances whites employ in the frontstage—which are typically multiracial spaces with diverse groups of people—and the backstage—which are private, comfortable, predominantly white spaces (Picca and Feagin 2007). To access whites in the backstage, researchers employ the following approaches: journaling, in-depth self-administered questionnaires, participant as observer with informants, and mixed methods or triangulation of ethnographic fieldwork, in-depth interviews, and content analysis.

JOURNALING

Journaling—one of the most common techniques—primarily takes two different approaches. McKinney's 2005 study analyzed autobiographies written by white college students on the way race affects their lives. McKinney prompted students to write about their first memories of learning about race, to consider whether race was one of the most important defining characteristics of their identity, to identify the messages they learned from family and friends about race, and to address the ways in which their race may affect their future, among several other topics. Students were encouraged to provide specific examples of stories and memories from their lives.

In contrast, Picca and Feagin's 2007 study asked college students at various universities, to spend several weeks recording "their observations of 'everyday events and conversations that deal with racial issues, images, and understandings'" (Picca and Feagin 2007, 31). Students were advised to provide specific "racial interactions, accounts, events, and comments" and to conceal the identifies of people in their journals (39). They were instructed to write journal entries even on the days that they were not involved in racial incidents. McKinney (2005) and Picca and Feagin (2007) recruited students for the project by contacting professors at universities and asking them to include their journal assignment as an extra credit opportunity for students (McKinney also offered the autographical assignment in her race and ethnicity courses). Faculty members at these various universities were provided with McKinney and Picca and Feagin's detailed instructions.

PARTICIPANT AS OBSERVER WITH INFORMANTS

The method of using participant as observer with informants requires researchers to identify potential student researchers who can naturally and seamlessly access and record interactions with family, friends, and acquaintances in the backstage. In this approach, the informant is both a source of research and a subject of research. Myers and Williamson (2001) and Myers (2005) used this approach in their study of race talk among college students. Researchers used campus advertisements to recruit voluntary informants. Most volunteers had taken a research methods course, typically held progressive attitudes, and questioned the racial hierarchy. Informants went through a detailed orientation process before going into the field to collect data. The orientation provided them with information on the data collection process and "operationalized race talk" so that they knew what to focus on. They were also provided with guidelines for how to interact in social settings. Informants were advised to take daily field notes, secretly record interactions, act naturally, not incite race talk (unless they would normally do so in these situations), create pseudonyms for recorded individuals (including themselves), and keep all field notes and recordings confidential.

MIXED METHODS/TRIANGULATION

The mixed methods/triangulation approaches are the most time-consuming techniques employed by backstage researchers. Hughey's 2011 study employed in-depth interviews, ethnographic field work, and content analysis to access the backstage discourse of white male members of a white nationalist group and an anti-racist group. Hughey wrote a letter to the leaders of each organization clearly identifying the purpose of his study: to observe the ways in which group members "interpreted racial identity" (Hughey 2015, 136). Hughey—who is a white male—was granted access to both groups, although he was seen as a "simultaneous insider and outsider"

(136). His ethnographic fieldwork consisted of one year in the field, and at least one day each week attending the group meetings of each organization. He strategically employed interviews with group members as a follow-up to attitudes and behaviors he observed from his fieldwork. Lastly, he conducted a content analysis of each groups' newsletters, emails, and other textual documents.

Embrick and Henricks (2015) examined "workers, supervisors, and lower-level managers" at a corporate baked goods business using participant observation and in-depth interviews. Embrick conducted the actual research in the field because his ambiguous racial phenotype allowed him to blend with backstage white spaces. After Embrick received permission to conduct the study from the company's human resources department, he gave the research participants a partial disclosure of the research project—omitting his intention to analyze race—to ensure that the data would not be compromised. Embrick spent six months in the field, four days each week, and took daily covert hand recordings of observations. Semi-structured, open-ended interviews were conducted *after* the participant observations for the purposes of deciding who would be interviewed, how the interviews would be structured, and identifying what observations needed follow-up.

IN-DEPTH SELF-ADMINISTERED QUESTIONNAIRES

This approach is relatively inexpensive and ideal for areas of inquiry that are difficult to infiltrate with journaling, for researchers of color who are unable to access the backstage via ethnographic fieldwork/participant observation because of their phenotype, and for researchers who do not have the resources or time to recruit informants. In-depth self-administered questionnaires provide respondents with anonymity, privacy, and comfort because questionnaires can be completed at their own pace and in the privacy of their homes. Slatton (2014) used this approach to access white men's attitudes about black women as potential relationship partners and to catalog their dating behavior with black women. Slatton (2014) advertised the questionnaire on a well-known web-based advertisement site, which allowed her to reach respondents from several regions and of varying ages and professions. To ensure quality responses, she ensured that questions were clear, concise, without academic jargon, and nonaccusatory. The questions were also open-ended and respondents were encouraged to provide specific details and personal examples. Before the questionnaire went live, Slatton (2014) conducted a test run of the questionnaire with a small group of white male college students to test its ease and accessibility.

FINDINGS AND CONTRIBUTIONS
OF BACKSTAGE STUDIES

Table 3.1 provides an overview of the design and contributions of key backstage studies. Each study provides evidence that old-fashioned, explicit forms of racism have not disappeared but have moved to backstage settings (Eliasoph 1999; Myers and Williamson 2001; McKinney 2005; Picca and Feagin 2007; Slatton 2014; Embrick and Henricks 2015). Contemporary stigmas and sanctions against overt racism leads whites to strategically *perform or do* race differently depending on the sociospatial settings. In the frontstage, many whites "present themselves as innocent of racism" and committed to color blindness and equality; yet in the backstage "the majority of whites still participate in openly racist performances . . . and do *not* define such performances as problematical" (Picca and Feagin 2007, 19, 22). The results from backstage studies not only identify the continued presence of old-fashioned expressions of racism but also contribute to our understanding of the machinations of racism in the backstage. In the following sections, I address the major contributions of the studies. (It is important to note that these contributions are not exhaustive.)

PASSIVE BYSTANDERS

Whites play a variety of roles in backstage racial performances. They may act as "protagonists, cheerleaders or bystanders" (Picca and Feagin 2007, 22). It is very rare that whites confront other whites who make racist statements or jokes in these backstage settings, even when they are offended (Picca and Feagin 2007; Eliasoph 1999). This finding is illustrated by Hannah, a journalist in Picca and Feagin's study, who wrote about a small house gathering where a friend made racist jokes and referred to blacks as "Porch Monkeys." When Hannah reflected on the event she lamented that this kind of joking really does bother me, but I don't know what to do about it. I know that I should probably stand up and say I feel uncomfortable when my friends tell jokes like that, but I know my friends would just get annoyed with me and say that they obviously don't mean anything by it.

SHIFTING RACIAL PERFORMERS

Whites change racial performances for the setting. In the frontstage, they may do a performance of color blindness, yet in the backstage, engage in overtly

Table 3.1 Summary of Key Backstage Studies on Racism and Intersections

Backstage Study	Method	Location	Subject	Sample Size	Findings
Embrick and Henricks (2015)	Mixed method-participant observation and in-depth interviews	Fieldwork at corporate business	Whites and nonwhites	38 (interviews)	34 instances of white race talk 50 uses of a racial slur
Slatton (2014)	In-depth self-administered questionnaires	Online	White males 18 over 50	134	Over 300 accounts of racial-gender discourse
Picca and Feagin (2007)	Journaling	Southern and Mid-Western Universities	College students, 18–25	626	9000 racial events
McKinney (2005)	Journaling	Southern and Northern Universities	College students	193	193 whiteness stories
Myers 2005/Myers and Williamson (2001)	Participant as observer via informants	Mid-Western University	College students	39 whites, 14 blacks, 7 Latinos, and 3 Asian-Americans	617 incidents of race talk
Hughey (2001)	Triangulation using ethnographic fieldwork, in-depth interviews, and content analysis	Fieldwork at nationalist and anti-racist organizations	White males 20–62	41 (interviews) 467 (content analysis)	Over 3000 accounts of racialized discourse.

racist behavior or express racialized attitudes. In the following illustration from Picca and Feagin (2007), Crystal details an experience with her friend's father at a dinner outing. The father explains why the particular northern city in which he lives in is such a great city:

> Her dad said that one of the reasons it was such a great city was because, unlike all the other big cities he could think of, there weren't a lot of black people running around. . . . I think the rest of us all thought it was a little weird he would say that, but none of us even talked about it after because we didn't want Sue to feel weird. We also know that parents were raised in a different time period and it just seems that parents, more often than kids in our generation, just have a different view of minorities. I don't think they are bad people for it, I just think they have to be a little more open-minded.

> After dinner, we went back to Sue's house to hang out and talk. One of Sue's roommates (Monica) is half black, half white. Sue's dad was very cordial and seemed to take real interest in what Monica talked about, He did not seem to be racist at all. He even told Monica that she should come out to visit Sue at their home sometime. (20)

This example clearly illustrates the father's adeptness at maneuvering racial performances depending on the social space. In the backstage, he shared clearly racialized views, yet in the frontstage with his daughter's roommate, he successfully performed color blindness.

DENIAL OF RACISM

Whites often rationalize the racist attitudes and behaviors of friends and relatives (Picca and Feagin 2007, 17). Their friends and family members, despite their statements and behaviors, are "not racist." Crystal—discussed in the previous quote—rationalizes the comment of her friend's father, by claiming that he was of a different generation and not a bad person. Similarly, the studies find that whites often justify their own racism by stating that they are not expressing racist attitudes but actual empirical experiences. Randy—a graduate school–educated respondent in Slatton's (2014) study—rationalized his racist comments in this way:

> I rode a bus with black females [and black males]. My interaction consisted of their rude obnoxious behavior, their foul smell and their disproportionate and ugly bodies. This is not a racist statement because I do not judge people based on their race. My statements are my FACTUAL experiences. (30–31)

REPRODUCTION OF WHITE IDENTITY

The studies reveal that the backstage is a private space in which whites, through isolated "hyper-segregated" interactions with each other, "reproduce" white identity "as a sense of group position in relation to nonwhite 'others' and the idealized white . . . self." Hence, the backstage is a place where white identity is performed and constituted (Hughey 2011, 133). Franklin, an informant in Hughey's 2011 study and member of a white nationalist group, illustrates how whites use private spaces to reproduce and normalize white superiority:

> Sure there is racism against blacks, it's against whites too. But you don't see whites running around shooting each other and getting high all the time. If prejudice really had that much of a social effect you would see it on both sides. Blacks can't help it . . . they are not as intelligent or moral, and it's unfair of us to expect them to be. Racial conflict is going to happen, prejudice is going to happen, . . . that's natural. But that this happens everywhere and whites succeed and blacks fail, well, that's a social experiment right then for you [laughing], the conclusions are right there. Whites are clearly superior and we deserve our own space. Maybe with time, if blacks had their own space and environment, that would somehow stabilize . . . . In the meantime they are screwed up, and it's not "racist" [emphasizing the word with "air quotes" as he spoke] of me to acknowledge that, yeah, to number one, acknowledge it and number two, act on it. That's not racist to say that black people have a criminal culture. (142)

RACIAL BOUNDARIES

Whites use the backstage to police and reaffirm white racial boundaries. In Myers and Williamson's (2001) study, a white informant's father made it clear that blacks and other people of color did not belong in their neighborhood:

> First my dad said something about the African American man and how he looked like a big hairy gorilla. Then he made a comment about the family of "dot-heads" that were walking up the driveway to their house. Then a car came with two men in it and he said, "First we have niggers, then dots, and now gay men—what else?" (14)

Picca and Feagin (2007, 147) found that whites also use nonverbal messages, such as eye winks and head nods, to police the "boundaries of backstage regions." Nonverbal messages signal that the backstage is no longer secure, because a frontstage region is nearby. Shannon, a journalist in their study, gives an example:

> I was standing in line at the fast food restaurant on Friday at about 1 pm with two of my female friends (both white and 20). There was a black family in front of us in line. One of my friends was trying to explain a contestant on a reality show she had seen the night before by saying, "The black girl . . . " My other friend's eyes widened and she motioned to the family in front of us, as if to say my friend should not be referring to someone by saying they're black, if people of the same race are in earshot. (146)

INTERSECTIONS

While many of the studies focused primarily on the racial discourse of whites in the backstage, studies by Slatton (2014) and Embrick and Henricks (2015) also analyzed the ways in which racist discourse shaped or intersected with classed and gendered discourses. These studies found substantial examples of gendered and classed racism. Slatton (2014) gives the following example from her study. In this quote, Lee, a white male respondent, describes black women in the following way:

> Just the term "black women" conjures up thoughts of an overweight dark-skinned loud poorly educated person with gold teeth yelling at somebody in public. I hope that doesn't make me racist but honestly that's the 1st thing I think of. (7)

Embrick and Henricks (2015) found that whites also use race and racial slurs to denote and denigrate the status (class) of certain types of work. In this example, Jeff—a long-haul transportation driver—engages in a backstage conversation with a white male coworker on completing a requested job:

Edward: Will you take those tires to the bakery?
Jeff: No. No I will not!
Edward: You won't? I'm just telling you what Mr. Smith said. He wants those to go back to the bakery.
Jeff: I'm not his nigger! I don't do nigger work! The god damn garage can get them with their small ass trucks.
Edward: So what do you want me to tell Mr. Smith?
Jeff: You tell him when he helps me, then I will help him. I'm not a fuckin' nigger! (173)

ATTITUDES AND BEHAVIORS

Traditional surveys and polls—which primarily only measure racial attitudes—often correspond attitudinal measures with hypothetical behaviors in abstract situations. A meta-analysis—conducted by Susan Fisk—of studies that examine correspondence between racial attitudes and discriminatory behavior found large variations (Pager and Quillan 2005). These results lead some researchers to caution against using survey measures of racial attitudes as proxies for discriminatory behaviors (Pager and Quillan 2005). Backstage methodological approaches offer an excellent advantage over traditional surveys because these studies allow researchers to capture attitudes *and* behaviors within concrete, real-life situations. Hence, backstage researchers do not have to use attitudinal measures as proxies for behaviors and generally do not have to rely on hypothetical situations.

LIMITATIONS AND CRITIQUES OF BACKSTAGE STUDIES

While backstage methodological approaches are quite adept at capturing attitudes and behaviors that are not as readily visible in the public domain of society, certain backstage techniques may be unable to account for or access implicit racial attitudes and behaviors. Social psychological studies find that people hold subconscious racial attitudes that they are unaware of. These types of attitudes are typically only accessed when they are primed by direct social contact with a person of color or other mechanisms (Greenwald, McGhee, and Schwartz 1998; Dasgupta et al. 2000; Devine 1989; Pager and Quillan 2005). Backstage studies that employ in-depth questionnaires or journaling may be unable to capture all of respondents' attitudes or emotions, since the respondent is not primed by a direct interaction. Hence, future backstage studies may consider incorporating techniques that will address this limitation.

Another potential limitation of certain backstage studies is the inability of researchers to follow up with respondents' statements or to address participants who may have omitted certain racial accounts (Picca and Feagin 2007). This issue is particularly relevant for studies that rely on in-depth questionnaires and journaling methods. To attend to this limitation, researchers that use these approaches typically encourage respondents to reflect on their responses during the journaling or questionnaire process. Studies that use mixed methods or triangulation are better able to follow up with the specific incidents or comments of their respondents. For example, in Hughey's 2001 study, he joined the anti-racist organization at an event on hate speech directed at black college students. During the event, several arguments ensued between people in interracial and intraracial groups. Hughey (2001) noted that at the end of the event a member of the anti-racist group turned to him and stated, "Why do they have to act like niggers?" This statement was in reference to two black men who argued at the event. Within a few days, Hughey was able to conduct a follow-up interview with the group member to gain valuable insight on the way in which this individual framed the event and his use of the racial slur.

Lastly, some may criticize backstage researchers for assuming that most forms and expressions of old-fashioned racism are in the backstage. However, most backstage researchers do not make this assumption and stress that frontstage racism is still quite viable in society; however, overt acts of racism appear to be more numerous in private, predominantly white, backstage spaces (Picca and Feagin 2007).

CONCLUSION

This chapter presents the value of backstage methodological approaches for identifying and analyzing the machinations of racism in contemporary society. The results of several key backstage studies on white racial attitudes and behaviors provide consistent evidence that old racist attitudes and inclinations have not declined in the way that traditional surveys on white racial attitudes suggest. New overt or subtle forms of racism have not replaced old-fashioned expressions of racism; instead, the bulk of these expressions have moved spatially and temporally. Whites know the spaces and the times they can participate in overt racist performances. And contrary to public sentiment, white supremacist and white nationalist events are not the only spaces where racial performances take place. The studies reveal that whites of varying ages, educational levels, socioeconomic status, and group affiliations (such as anti-racist organizations) *do* racist performances—which at times intersect with sexist and classist performances—in the backstage.

Importantly, backstage methodological research contributes to our overall understanding of the ways in which racial performances in private all-white social spaces reaffirms white identity and "sustains and buttresses" the "system of oppression" that such performances derive from (Picca and Feagin 2007, 7; Hughey 2001).

BIBLIOGRAPHY

American Civil Liberties Union. 2013. "The War on Marijuana in Black and White." New York: American Civil Liberties Union. Accessed September, 19 2013. https://www.aclu.org/files/assets/aclu-thewaronmarijuana-rel2.pdf.

Bertrand, Marianne, and Sendhil Mullainathan. 2004. "Are Emily and Greg More Employable than Lakisha and Jamal? A Field Experiment on Labor Market Discrimination." *American Economic Review* 94(4): 991–1013.

Bonilla-Silva, Eduardo. 2002. "The Linguistics of Color Blind Racism: How to Talk Nasty about Blacks without Sounding 'Racist.'" *Critical Sociology* 28(1–2): 41–64.

Bonilla-Silva, Eduardo. 2003. *Racism without Racists: Color-Blind Racism and the Persistence of Racial Inequality in the United States.* Lanham, MD: Rowman & Littlefield.

Bonilla-Silva, Eduardo. 2011. "The Sweet Enchantment of Color-Blind Racism in Obamerica." *Annals of the American Academy of Political and Social Science* 634(1): 190–206.

Bobo, Lawrence D., James R. Kluegel, and Ryan A. Smith. 1997. "Laissez-Fair Racism." In *Racial Attitudes in the 1990s*, edited by Steven Tuch and Jack K. Martin, 15–24. Westport, CT: Praeger.

Carr Priyanka B., Dweck, Carol S., and Kristin Pauker. 2012. "Prejudiced Behavior without Prejudice? Beliefs about the Malleability of Prejudice Affect Interracial Interactions." *Journal of Personality and Social Psychology* 103(3): 452–471.

Center for Constitutional Rights. 2012. "Stop and Frisk: The Human Impact." New York: Center for Constitutional Rights. Accessed September 19, 2013. http://stopansfrisk .org/the-humanimpact-report.pdf.

Dasgupta, Nilanjana, Debbie E. McGhee, Anthony G. Greenwald, and Mahzarin R. Banaji. 2000. "Automatic Preference for White Americans: Eliminating the Familiarity Explanation." *Journal of Experimental Social Psychology* 36: 316–328.

Dovidio John F., and Samuel L. Gaertner. 2004. "Aversive Racism." *Advances in Experimental Social Psychology* 36: 1–51.

Devine, Patricia. 1989. "Stereotypes and Prejudice: Their Automatic and Controlled Components." *Journal of Personality and Social Psychology* 56: 5–18.

Devine, Patricia G. and Andrew J. Elliot. 1995. "Are Racial Stereotypes Really Fading? The Princeton Trilogy Revisited." *Personality and Social Psychology Bulletin* 21: 1139–50.

DiTomaso, Nancy. 2013. *The American Non-Dilemma: Racial Inequality without Racism.* New York: Sage Foundation.

Eberhardt Jennifer L., Phillip Atiba Goff, Valerie J. Purdie, and Paul G. Davies. 2004. "Seeing Black: Race, Crime, and Visual Processing." *Journal of Personality and Social Psychology* 87(6): 876–893.

Eliasoph, Nina. 1999. "'Everyday Racism' in a Culture of Political Avoidance: Civil Society, Speech, and Taboo." *Social Problems* 46(4): 479–502.

Embrick, David, and Kasey Henricks. 2015. "Two-Faced-isms: Racism at Work and How Race Discourse Shapes Classtalk and Gendertalk." *Language Sciences* 52: 165—175.

Emerson, Michael O., and Christian Smith. 2000. *Divided by Faith: Evangelical Religion and the Problem of Race in America.* New York: Oxford University Press.

Feliciano, Cynthia, Belinda Robnett, and Golnaz Komaie. 2009. "Gendered Racial Exclusion among White Internet Daters." *Social Science Research* 38(1): 39–54.

Glover, Scott. 2009. "Donald Sterling to Pat $2.725 Million to Settle Housing Discrimination Lawsuit." *Los Angeles Times*, November 3. Accessed June 1, 2016. http://latimesblogs.latimes.com/lanow/2009/11/donald-sterling-to-pay-2725-million-to-settle-housing-discrimination-lawsuit.html.

Goffman, Erving. 1959. *The Presentation of Self in Everyday Life*. Garden City, NY: Doubleday.

Greenwald, Anthony, Debbie E. McGhee, and Jordan Schwartz. 1998. "Measuring Individual Differences in Implicit Cognition: The Implicit Association Test." *Journal of Personality and Social Psychology* 74(6):1464–1480.

Hatchette, Shirley, and Howard Schuman. 1975. "White Respondents and Race-of-Interviewer Effects." *Public Opinion Quarterly* 39: 523–528.

Henry, P. J., and David O. Sears. 2002. "The Symbolic Racism 2000 Scale." *Political Psychology* 23(2): 253–283.

Hughey, Matthew W. 2011. "Backstage Discourse and the Reproduction of White Masculinities." *The Sociological Quarterly* 52(1):132–153.

Jacobsen, Michael H., and Soren Kristiansen. 2015. *The Social Thought of Erving Goffman*. Thousand Oaks, CA: Sage Publications.

Jones, Jeffery M. 2005. "Most Americans Approve of Interracial Dating." *Gallup*. October 7. http://www.gallup.com/poll/19033/most-americans-approve-interracial-dating.aspx.

Jones, Jeffery M. 2011. "Record High 86% Approve of Black-White Marriages." *Gallup*. September 12. http://www.gallup.com/poll/149390/record-high-approve-black-white-marriages.aspx.

Kinder, Donald, and David O. Sears. 1981. "Prejudice and Politics: Symbolic Racism Versus Racial Threats to the Good Life." *Journal of Personality and Social Psychology* 40: 414–431.

LaPiere, Richard T. 1934. "Attitudes vs Actions." *International Journal of Epidemiology* 39(1): 7–11.

Leach, Colin Wayne. 2005. "Against the Notion of a 'New Racism.'" *Journal of Community and Applied Social Psychology* 15: 432–455.

Lin Ken-Hou, and Jennifer Lundquist. 2013. "Mate Selection in Cyberspace: The Intersection of Race, Gender, and Education." *American Journal of Sociology* 119(1): 183–215.

Massey, Douglass S. and Nancy A. Denton. 1993. *American Apartheid: Segregation and the Making of the Underclass*. Cambridge, MA: Harvard University Press.

McKinney, Karyn D. 2005. *Being White: Stories of Race and Racism*. New York: Routledge.

Mendes, Wendy Berry, Jim Blascovich, Brian Lickel, and Sarah Hunter. 2002. "Challenge and Threat during Social Interactions with White and Black Men." *Personality and Social Psychology* 28(7): 939–952.

Myers, Kristen A. 2005. *Racetalk: Racism Hiding in Plainsight*. Lanham, MD: Rowman & Littlefield.

Myers, Kristen A., and Passion Williamson. 2001. "Race Talk: The Perpetuation of Racism through Private Discourse." *Race and Society* 4(1): 3–26.

Murakawa, Naomi, and Katherine Beckett. 2010. "The Penology of Racial Innocence: The Erasure of Racism in the Study and Practice of Punishment." *Law &
Society Review* 44(3–4): 695–730.

National Research Council. 2004. Measuring Racial Discrimination. Panel on Meth-
ods for Assessing Discrimination, Committee on National Statistics, Division of
Behavior and Social Sciences and Education, edited by Rebecca M. Blank, Marilyn
Dabady, and Constance F. Citro. Washington, DC: The National Academic Press.

New York Civil Liberties Union. 2013. "Stop and Frisk Data." New York: New
York Civil Liberties Union. Accessed September 19, 2013. http://www.nyclu.org/
content/stop-and-frisk-data.

Nittle, Nadra Kareem. 2014. "Transcript of Alleged Donald Sterling V. Stiviano
Recording." About News. Accessed September 15, 2015. http://www.racerelations.
about.com.

Pager, Devah. 2003. "The Mark of a Criminal Record." *American Journal of Sociology* 108(5): 937–975.

Pager, Devah. 2007. "The Use of Field Experiments for Studies of Employment
Discrimination: Contributions, Critiques, and Directions for the Future." *ANNALS*
609: 104–33.

Pager, Devah, and Lincoln Quillan. 2005. "Walking the Talk? What Employers Say
versus What They Do." *American Sociological Review* 70(3): 355–380.

Phua, Voon C., and Gayle Kaufman. 2005. "The Crossroads of Race and Sexuality:
Date Selection Among Men in Internet 'Personal' Ads." *Journal of Family* (24):
981–994.

Picca, Leslie Houts, and Joe R. Feagin. 2007. *Two-Faced Racism: Whites in the Backstage and Frontstage*. New York: Routledge.

Qian, Zhenchao, and Daniel T. Litcher. 2007. "Social Boundaries and Marital
Assimilation: Interpreting Trends in Racial and Ethnic Intermarriage." *American
Sociological Review* 72: 68–94.

Richeson, Jennifer, and Sophie Devine Trawalter. 2005. "On the Categorization of
Admired and Disliked Exemplers of Admired and Disliked Racial Groups." *Journal of Personality and Social Psychology* 89(4): 517–530.

Robnett, Belinda, and Cynthia Feliciano. 2011. "Patterns of Racial-Ethnic Exclusion
by Internet Daters." *Social Forces* 89(3): 807–828.

Schuman, Howard, Charlottee Steech, Lawrence Bobo, and Maria Krysan. 2001.
Racial Attitudes in America: Trends and Interpretations. Rev. ed. Cambridge, MA:
Harvard University Press.

Shelton, J. Nicole. 2003. "Interpersonal Concerns in Social Encounters between
Majority and Minority Group Members." *Group Processes and Intergroup Relations* 6: 171–185.

Slatton, Brittany. 2014. *Mythologizing Black Women: Unveiling White Men's Racist
and Sexist Deep Frame*. New York: Routledge.

Smith, Jacob. 2008. *Vocal Tracks: Performance and Sound Media*. Berkeley: University of California Press.

Sudman, Seymour, and Norman M. Bradburn. 1982. *Asking Questions: A Practical
Guide to Questionnaire Design*. San Fransisco: Jossey-Bass.

Supphellen, M., O. A. Kvitastein, and S. T. Johanesen. 1997. "Projective Questioning and Ethnic Discrimination: A Procedure for Measuring Employer Bias." *Public Opinion Quarterly* 61: 208–224.

Tarman, Christopher, and David O. Sears. 2005. "The Conceptualization and Measurement of Symbolic Racism." *Journal of Politics* 67: 731–761.

Trawalter, Sophie, and Jennifer A. Richeson. 2008. "Let's Talk about Race, Baby! When Whites' and Blacks' Interracial Contact Experiences Diverge." *Journal of Experimental Social Psychology* 44(4): 1214–1217.

U.S. Census Bureau. 2010. *Table 60. Married Couples by Race and Hispanic Origin of Spouses*. Washington, DC: U.S. Government Printing Office.

Watkins-Hayes, Celeste. 2009. Book Review, "Two Faced Racism: Whites in the Backstage and Frontstage." *Social Forces* 87(4): 2183—2185.

Yancey, George. 2007. "Homogamy Over the Net: Using Internet Advertisements to Discover Who Interracially Dates." *Journal of Social and Personal Relationships* 24: 913–930.

Chapter 4

"Girls Can't Play No Ball"

The Invisibility of Black Woman Athletes in Film

Drew Brown

Film and sport are institutions that often reflect the broader US society. However, in both institutions, intersectional oppression has marginalized Black women. As a result, Black women athletes (BWAs) are extremely underrepresented in film, especially when compared to White men, White women, and Black men. In addition, according to Africana womanist theory, the few BWA characters who do exist are missing many elements found in culturally authentic Africana women (Hudson-Weems 1993). Much of Black women's self-development and identity construction is influenced by the way Black women are portrayed in films. The nonexistent and inaccurate images exemplify the multidimensional oppression that continuously and publicly obscures Black women to subordinate social roles.

White male athletes are the protagonists in a disproportionate number of films that carry a heavy sports theme such as *Rocky*, *Rudy*, *Slap Shot*, and *Varsity Blues*. These roles have been developed with many positive elements. Black male athletes are also been the featured protagonists in many sports films, though often featuring stereotypical assumptions about their super-human athleticism. For example, they are found in fiction films such as *Any Given Sunday, Jerry McGuire, Above the Rim, The Program, Hoop Dreams, Friday Night Lights,* and *White Men Can't Jump.* There are also a significant amount of biographical films centered on real Black male athletes such as Jackie Robinson, Jesse Owens, Michael Orr, Muhammad Ali, and Ruben "Hurricane" Carter. Conversely, there are very few biographical films that tell the story of real-life BWAs. The movie *The Longshots* is based on the story of Jasmine Plummer, who was the first Black girl as well as the first girl-quarterback to play in the Pop Warner youth tournament. Also, the Olympic gold medal gymnast Gabby Douglas had a biopic, *The Gabby Douglas Story*, produced as a Lifetime original movie. There are numerous other

BWAs who are well deserving of a film: Wilma Rudolph, Althea Gibson, Ora Washington, Alice Coachman, and Florence "Flo-Jo" Griffith Joyner.

In addition to the abundance of films that are centered on male athletes, there are also a number of movies that highlight White *female* athletes such as *Million Dollar Baby, A League of Their Own, Quarterback Princess, Personal Best, Blue Crush,* and *Double Teamed.* Other films feature White female athletes playing on gender-integrated teams such as *Mighty Ducks* and *Little Giants.* Highlighting women as the protagonists in films—an arena where men have traditionally dominated—has proven to be a struggle. The presence of women in a socially demarcated "male realm" jeopardizes the assumptions of masculinity that are supported by "exclusively male" activities such as sports. However, since the passing of Title IX in 1972, White woman athletes have an increased presence in sports and film. The same cannot be said for BWAs.

The invisibility of BWAs in movies is supported by the long legacy of intersectional—race and gender—oppression that face Black women in sports and film. There are no box office movies that feature a BWA as the sole protagonist. The movies *Love & Basketball* and *The Longshots* show BWAs as leading characters, but each film has them alongside a Black male coprotagonist. *Love & Basketball* depicts the relationship between two life-long friends who share a deep love for basketball and each other. The story line captures the stereotypes associated with a talented BWA who attempts to navigate between athletics and her everyday life while facing the challenges and expectations due to her gender. The relationship she shares with her male counterpart is saturated with many elements of Africana womanism. However, like all of the other movies that present BWAs, many elements of an Africana woman remain absent.

There are other films that exhibit BWAs as secondary characters such as *Bring It On*, a film about White cheerleaders who stole routines from an inner city squad composed predominately of people of color; *Jawanna Mann,* which features a Black male athlete character who performs as a BWA for unethical reasons; and *Higher Learning,* where a BWA plays a small but significant role in the struggles of a Black male student-athlete dealing with racism at his college. Unfortunately, many of the BWAs in these films maintain the same culturally inauthentic and negative characteristics that generally plague depictions of Black women in film.

In film, as in US society, there exists an intersectional oppression based on race and gender reflected in the portrayal of the Black woman. More specifically, the character development of BWAs resembles the general treatment of Black women throughout the US film industry. Some roles played by Black women are lacking dignity (Thompson 2013). Furthermore, Black actresses voice discontent with their inability to find complex character roles that do not reinforce negative stereotypes of Black women. J. J. Royster (2000) asserts that Black women are constantly subjected to standards set and monitored by others who disregard and ignore their best interests. These barriers leave Black women underrepresented as movie characters that promote a sense of self, racial, and gender empowerment. While positive images of Black women are scarce, they are overrepresented as caregivers, sex addicts, or enraged characters.

In this chapter, I use an Africana studies approach, which is interdisciplinary and culturally subjective, to examine the intersectional oppression of Black women, the race and gender politics of sport, and the culturally inappropriate depictions of BWAs. I do this by outlining Black women's intersectional struggle in sports and film and analyzing the few existing examples of BWAs in film using an Africana womanist theoretical framework. In the end, what is found is the need for more culturally appropriate movie characters that represent authentic Africana womanist athletes. I also suggest that this can be accomplished partially by increasing the number of Black female movie directors who are familiar with struggles and identity of the BWAs.

AFRICANA WOMANISM

As a result of the intersectional challenges that continue to plague Black women, it is important to examine this phenomenon in a way that is culturally appropriate, highlights the perspective of Black women, and considers intersectionality when addressing oppression. Black women scholars have developed several theoretical frameworks that acutely interpret a Black woman's American perspective (Banks-Wallace 2000). In this chapter, Africana womanism is utilized to examine the ways in which BWAs are subjected to racial and gender oppression that inhibits them from being culturally affirmative lead characters in film.

Feminism appeals to many scholars looking to articulate the linkages between the oppression of their gender to the racism they experience. There have been many significant contributors to Black feminism such as Patricia Hill Collins, Toni Cade Bambara, Akasha (Gloria T.) Hull, Barbara Smith, Michele Wallace, Angela Davis, Kimberle Crenshaw, Toni Morrison, Alice Walker, Audre Lorde, and other Black women who helped to develop a self-defined, collective Black women's standpoint about black womanhood (Collins 1996). According to Michael Eric Dyson, the term "Black feminist" challenges the accepted and unquestioned ideas of Black racial solidarity that ignore internal gender oppression, especially Black nationalist and cultural pluralist frameworks (Collins 1996, 13).

In contemporary discourse, there continues to be much debate about whether the term "Black feminism" is most appropriate (Collins 1996). Clenora Hudson-Weems (2000) claims that many adopted a feminist paradigm because of the absence of a more suitable framework. She also states that some of them are now reexamining the foundational origin and historical reality of the movement. Knowing the anti-Black history of feminism and its white-women-centered framework, using the term "Black feminism" seems inappropriate when addressing the concerns of Black women. It is unwise to simply infuse race into existing theoretical frameworks that are used to examine the characters of White athletes. The multidimensional oppression facing BWAs cannot be simplified through theories that are meant for examining their White counterparts. The differences are too significant to overlook. The cultural differences and history of enslavement, oppression, and racial treatment create too many phenomenological differences. Thus a more appropriate theory should be utilized. Black psychologist Julia Hare voiced her rejection of feminism by stating,

> Women who are calling themselves Black feminists need another word that describes what their concerns are. Black Feminism is not a word that describes the plight of Black women. The white race has a woman problem because the women were oppressed. Black people have a man and woman problem because Black men are as oppressed as their women. (Hudson-Weems 2000)

Hare is unaware or not acknowledging the discourse that has been developed to address her concerns. Black women liberation theories and terms that currently exist include womanism and Africana womanism. Some scholars prefer the term "womanism" as a way to disassociate from the racist White women who founded the feminist movement. Although these terms are often used interchangeably in much of the literature (Banks-Wallace 2000), it is important to understand the fundamental and significant differences between the theories and utilize the ones most appropriate.

Barbara Omolade argues, "black feminism is sometimes referred to as womanism because both are concerned with struggles against sexism and racism by Black women who are themselves part of the black community's efforts to achieve equity and liberty" (Omolade 1995, xx). Likewise, Alice Walker defines the term "womanist" in her book *In Search of Our Mothers' Gardens* by stating that a "womanist" is "a black feminist or feminist of color" (Walker 1983, xi). Here Walker describes the interchangeability of the two terms and sees both as theories supporting Black women's self-definition and self-determination (Collins 1996, 9–10). Although the framework of womanism is most associated with Alice Walker's definition of the term, it has at least two additional theorists who originally conceived and developed their own distinct form of womanism independent of each other: Chikwenye Okonjo Ogunyemi and Clenora Hudson-Weems (Karenga and Tembo 2012, 34).

Karenga urges an African-centered form of womanism that carries a long, diverse, and rich tradition with origins in African culture (Karenga and Tembo 2012, 33) Likewise, Hudson-Weems stresses the need for "Africana scholars to create and utilized paradigms and theoretical frameworks" that come from within their own cultural ethics and philosophy (Hudson-Weems 1997, 79). Weems criticizes Black feminism by asserting that Africana womanism is

> Neither an outgrowth nor an addendum to feminism, Africana Womanism is not Black feminism, Africana feminism, or Walker's Womanism that some Africana women have come to embrace. Africana Womanism is an ideology created and designed for all woman of African descent; it is grounded in African culture, and therefore, it necessarily focuses on the unique experiences, struggles, needs, and desires of Africana Black. . . . The primary goal of Africana Black, then, is to create their own criteria for assessing their realities, both in thought and in action. (Hudson-Weems 1993, 24, 50)

Like most other African women liberation theories, Africana womanism challenges the legitimacy of Eurocentric research that does not empower Black women (Ferguson 2015, 40). Africana womanism encompasses the philosophic and cultural elements of Afrocentricity. It must be stated that merely viewing Africana phenomena through a racial lens is still not sufficient enough for an adequate understanding of BWAs. In fact, race is only one aspect of Afrocentricity. Historian Gerald Early argues that Afrocentricity is "that ideological epoxy meant to bind black people more as a matter of culture and spirit than of race" (Vertinsky and Captain 1998, 21). Afrocentric scholar Molefi Asante adds clarity by stating, "Afrocentricity is African genius and African values created, decreated, reconstructed, and derived from our history and our experiences in our best interests. It is the clarity and focus through which black people must see the world in order to escalate" (Asante 1987, 180).

Africana womanism is based in Afrocentric thought that focusing specifically on the experiences, struggles, needs, and desires of Africana women of the African diaspora (Hudson-Weems 1993, 154–155). Hudson-Weems describes the meaning behind the term "Africana womanism":

> Its primary goal . . . is to create their [Africana Black's] own criteria for assessing their realities, both in thought and in action. The first part of the coinage, Africana, identifies the ethnic background of the woman being considered, and this reference to her ethnicity, establishing her cultural identity, relates directly to her ancestry and land base-Africa. The second part of the term, womanism,

in addition to taking us back to the rich legacy of African womanhood, recalls Sojourner Truth's powerful impromptu speech "And Ain't I a Woman?" The term "woman," and by extension "womanism," is far more appropriate than the term "female" (feminism), as only a female of the human race can be a woman. "Female," on the other hand, can refer to a member of the animal or plant kingdom, as well as to a member of the human race. Finally, in electronic and mechanical terminology, there is a female counterbalance to the male cor-relative. Hence, terminology derived from the word "woman" is more suitable and more specific when naming a group of the human race. (Hudson-Weems 1993, 50)

Africana womanism is the most suitable theoretical framework for this essay because it provides a culturally appropriate framework for analyz-ing BWA characters, highlighting the intersectional oppression facing Black women and prioritizing the Black woman perspective. This analy-sis will utilize Africana womanism to identify the stereotyping of BWAs and examine racist characterizations and inauthentic representations of them. In her seminal work, *Africana Womanism: Reclaiming Ourselves*, Hudson-Weems identifies eighteen themes that should guide the analysis of the Africana woman experience. She describes the Africana womanist as (1) a self-namer, (2) a self-definer, (3) family centered, (4) genuine in sisterhood, (5) strong, (6) in concert with the Africana man in struggle, (7) whole, (8) authentic, (9) a flexible role player, (10) respected, (11) recognized, (12) spiritual, (13) male compatible, (14) respectful of elders, (15) adaptable, (16) ambitious, (17) mothering, and (18) nurturing. While all of these characteristics are considered, only some are extensively fea-tured in this analysis. In order to gain a full understanding of the BWA identity and experience, it must be contextualized in the struggle for Black women.

MULTIDIMENSIONAL OPPRESSION OF BLACK WOMEN

Many writers posit that Black women are rendered "invisible" (Banks-Wallace 2000; DePauw 1997; Fryberg and Townsend 2008; Hudson-Weems 2000; King 1988; Sesko and Biernat, 2010). Amanda K. Sesko and Monica Biernat define "invisibility" as "an absence of, or erroneous representations of, oppressed groups and/or individuals" (2010, 357). In other words, when addressing gender or race, Black women face a lack of individualism or lack of differentiation from their White female or Black male group members. Black women are not seen as exemplars of the various groups to which they belong (Sesko and Biernat 2010; Fryberg and Townsend 2008).

Being both women and Black people, Black women have experienced a deep history of simultaneous denigration (Banks-Wallace 2000). Many scholars call this phenomenon the "double jeopardy" of gender and racial oppression. Deborah King argues that Black women are often subjected to "multiple-jeopardy" because they belong to multiple subordinated groups. She posits, "Unfortunately, most applications of the concepts of double and triple jeopardy have been overly simplistic in assuming that the relationships among the various discriminations are merely additive" (King 1988, 47). In other words, the dual and systematic discriminations of racism and sexism remain pervasive and compounded when additional identities such as sexuality, class, or athletic participation are considered. King further claims that the Black female experience is not simply a sum of the woman experience and the Black experience but a multiplicity of the two (and additional identities), creating unique experiences that are similar in ways and different in other ways than that of non-Black women within their subordinated groups (King 1988). Kimberle Crenshaw identifies the experiences of subordinate people who belong to multiple subordinate groups as "intersectional oppression" (Crenshaw 1991). For BWAs, the oppressive forces behind their limited characterization in film are led by gendered forms of racism or patriarchal White supremacy.

Jim Sidanius and Rosemary C. Veniegas suggest that while Black women are subject to gender-specific discrimination in a patriarchal society, Black men are the primary targets of racial discrimination. In other words, Black women may face less "targeted" forms of racial discrimination but more sexualized attacks than Black men (Sesko and Biernat 2010, 347; Sidanius and Veniegas 2000). Likewise, in film, much of the attention is focused on the experiences or oppression of Black men. For example, the film *Birth of a Nation* illustrated the racist attitudes of many Whites. However, the majority of the film and the criticism were devoted to the way Black men were portrayed as evil predators. The National Association for the Advancement of Colored People (NAACP) was elevated to a position of national stature after organizing in cities across the country against the film. However, little, if any, attention was paid to the film's portrayal or invisibility of Black women (Wallace 2003). Both the civil rights movement and Black power movement have been criticized for focusing their fight of oppression toward issues that generally impact Black males. While Black women experience anti-Black sentiment, their struggle with forms of racism based on their gender has been minimized.

Movies about Black women characters are rarely developed from a Black woman's perspective. Most movie writers rely on the "oppositional gaze" that constructs detrimental societal images and expectations of Black women. This gaze characterizes Black women as dominant, aggressive, sexually promiscuous, vulgar, and loud (Thomas 2004; West 1995). The consequence of these depictions is the characterizing of Black women that seldom exhibits positive or cultural aspects of Africana culture, shows a resistance to racial-gender oppressions, promotes the traditional characteristics of Black women, or celebrates the cultural identity of Black women.

Black adolescents are challenged with the task of negotiating positive ideals of self while being presented false or misrepresented images of Black womanhood (Muhammad and McArthur 2015). Some scholars argue that the distorted images of Black femininity that derive from a history of stereotypes that include the mammy, jezebel, and Sapphire have pervaded contemporary media sources (West 1995; Thomas 2004). The current qualitative interview study examined literate interpretations of current media representations depicting Black girlhood from eight adolescent girls. Findings show that participants viewed the images of Black females as angry, loud, violent, and sexualized. When assumptions and ideas of Black women are further complicated by their involvement in sports, positive image formation of BWAs is imperative because the lack of positive images of Black women can be connected to the self-esteem of Black girls. Likewise, culturally underdeveloped BWA characters in film will leave a lasting impact on Black girls. When assessing the invisibility and analyzing BWAs in film, it is important to examine this phenomenon through a theoretical frame that will address the multidimensional oppression of BWAs—and also honor the greatness of their agency.

BLACK WOMEN ATHLETES IN SPORTS

Historically, women were discouraged from participating in sports, and those who did were viewed as manly, especially Black women (Lansbury 2014). Sports have historically operated as a space that models hegemonic masculinity in US society; it is a place where characteristics of masculinity and manhood are constructed and perpetuated. The mere presence of Black women as athletes in US-produced films stretches the traditional gender roles and norms that limit social conceptions of manhood, womanhood, and gender-appropriate activities. During the early half of the twentieth century, many people did not believe sports were the place for women because it was a considered a "masculine activity" (Lansbury 2014). Some even claimed that the physical nature of sport jeopardized the biological harmony of women and damaged their reproduction ability (Hall 2001). BWAs' womanhood has been continuously challenged and compared to White women. The speech "Ain't I a Woman" by Sojourner Truth illustrates the long legacy of Black women's struggle for womanhood. In her speech, Truth lays out several points that show how Black women are encouraged to adhere to a culturally foreign model of womanhood that most often does not match their history and experiences. Black women often fail to meet, or are denied, the form of womanhood promoted by the dominant group. Thus, White supremacy maintains social exclusivity and the hegemony of White womanhood progresses. In addition, BWAs' participation in athletics further alienates them from the rigid social conceptions of White womanhood.

The contention between BWAs' athleticism and femininity is evident in the 1931 writings of Ivora King, a columnist for the *Baltimore Afro American*, who stated that "the girl who is too athletic is on the wrong track to becoming a wife. . . . Men want women all women . . . being too athletic, and consequently too mannish, prevents her from being" (Vertinsky and Captain 1998, 540). Even though BWAs continued to develop into great athletes through the 1930s and 1940s, non-BWAs like King still considered them overly manly. Because of the defeminizing of BWAs, Black coaches, journalists, and community leaders of the 1930–1960s did all they could to feminize the image of BWAs. Edward Temple was the star track and field coach for the Tennessee State Tigerbelles during the 1960s. He demanded that his female athletes follow a dress code. He once told a reporter, "I tell them that they are young ladies first, track girls second. I want them well-groomed all the time, even when they run. And nobody takes their picture unless their hair is combed and their face is fixed" (Lansbury 2014, 135).

Since women athletes have become more socially acceptable than in previous generations, the number of sports leagues and teams available to White women highly outnumber those available to BWAs, especially after the passing of Title IX in 1972. Title IX is an initiative that was established to create gender equality that mandated universities to have an equal number of athletes and resources between men and women (Rhoden 2004). The act states, "No person in the United States shall, on the basis of sex, be excluded from participation in, be denied the benefits of, or be subjected to discrimination under any education program or activity" (Ahmed 2004, 361). This required some universities to develop new teams and provide scholarships for more female athletes. While some may argue that Title IX has increased the opportunities for female athletes to acquire a college education through athletic scholarships, Title IX has mainly increased "gender-appropriate" sports that are dominated by *White* female athletes such as field hockey, lacrosse, and cheerleading (Pearson 2001; Rhoden 2004).

Even though female athletes are encouraged to participate in "gender-appropriate" sports, structural forces sometimes keep BWAs from accessing them. Some sports, such as field hockey, lacrosse, swimming, tennis, and golf, require equipment that is not often available for racial or economic reasons (Holland 2002). For sports like swimming and tennis specifically, accessibility to proper facilities is a major issue for BWAs. This lack of resources is illustrated in *Bring It On* and *The Longshots* where the BWAs are initially unable to participate in the national championship competitions because of the financial costs that the team was unable to meet.

Although economic and accessibility issues have hinder many Black women from participating in sports that require lots of resources, they excel in sports like basketball and track that require little equipment and have facilities available in low economic status areas. Even though basketball and track were once not considered "gender-appropriate" sports for women, BWAs have always dominated in them. To a certain extent, this has been accepted by the dominant society, which has always challenged Black women's womanhood regardless of their participation in basketball and track.

BLACK WOMEN ATHLETES IN FILM

Bring It On is a cheerleading movie that, for some, is not a sports movie because cheerleading is not associated with masculinity but rather with femininity (Grindstaff and West 2006). Not viewing cheerleading as a sport maintains the exclusivity of male- and masculine-dominated sports. Cheerleading, in its traditional form, mirrors the social status often given to women in the broader society. Cheerleaders, and women in general, are not considered the central or leading participants but rather are relegated to the sidelines where they support the efforts of males. The issue of objectification is also present cheerleading. The only time cheerleaders get to occupy the central space is when the male athletes take a break and the cheerleaders are used to bring entertainment and titillation for the male-dominated audiences.

This description of cheerleaders and women is limiting and devalues their role. For example, they are expected to dress in short skirts or shorts. This is especially an issue for BWA who have a history of being sexualized. The attempt to feminize the image of BWAs resulted in the emergence of a more acceptable but hypersexualized portrayal of BWAs by the dominant society (Lansbury 2014). Contrastingly, the BWAs in *Bring It On* centered on their own goals; they are never shown on the fringes of a male-dominated sporting activity, but always at the center of the performances where they take an active role in bringing success to their school. Even though this movie is based on competitive cheerleading, they cannot avoid the stereotypical, sexualized image that cheerleaders carry.

Many of the sports movies that feature women highlight sports dominated by White women. *Bend it Like Beckham* is a movie about woman's soccer team, and *Bring It On* is a cheerleading movie. Moreover, many of the movies about sports that BWAs dominate, such as women's boxing and basketball, do not feature BWA characters either. An example of this is the film *Double Team,* about two White female friends who work to reach the Women's National Basketball Association (WNBA).

The few films that focus on BWAs are written and directed by non-Black women. The misguided and Eurocentric framework that promotes a false uniformity of Black women's lives often portrays myths and stereotypes that misrepresent BWAs (Vertinsky and Captain 1998). One of the more egregious portrayals of a BWA is in the film *Juwanna Mann,* written by Bradley Allenstein. The movie features a Black male basketball player who cross-dresses as a woman in order to play in the WNBA. Not only does this character not represent an authentic BWAs, this character's disingenuous motives undermine the struggle of the transgender and other queer communities. This movie could be guilty of having a gendered version of Blackface as the central plot. Even the less egregious depictions of BWAs in other movies still fail to produce an authentic image of a BWA. Moreover, they fail to highlight Africana womanist characteristics such as being a nurturer, respectful of elders, and spiritual.

Some elements of an Africana woman are found sparingly in films featuring BWA characters, even if the writers did not intend for them to be interpreted as such. However, in all of the movies examined, much of the focus is on gender inequality. While gender equality is a major aspect of Africana womanism, Hudson-Weems (2000) argues that racism alone is a bigger influence on the lives of Black people than classism and sexism. She argues, "For the majority of Black women, racism has been the most important obstacle in the acquisition of basic needs for survival" (Hudson-Weems 2000, 19). She later concludes, "Race and class biases are the key issues for non-Whites and must be resolved even before gender issues if there is any hope for human survival" (Hudson-Weems 2000, 41). Contrary to Africana womanism, racism, race, or Black identity are very rarely touched on in media portrayals of BWAs. Many of the films focus on the gender identity among BWAs but fail to produce or develop a conscious African/Black identity within the characters.

Issues of gender are placed at the forefront of films like *Love & Basketball* and *The Longshots.* For example, *Love & Basketball* begins with a group of adolescent boys playing basketball in the driveway when the new neighbor joins them. After competing strong, the boys find out that the new player is a girl. The best of the boy ballers shouts out, "girls can't play no ball." He is suggesting that girls are not adequate to play, at least with or in comparison to the boys, in a competitive way. In later scene, Monica points out to her male best friend and fellow baller the double standards facing woman athletes. She says, "You get in a guy's face, and talk smack, and you get a pat on the ass. But because I'm a female, I get told to 'act like a lady.' She declared, 'I'm a ball player!'" This display of self-naming—Nommo—is an important part of African cosmology and Africana womanism (Hudson-Weems 2000, 55). Her declaration that men are awarded for aggression and women are scolded for it is a call for equality and shows her resistance to the double standards and gender-specific reproaching of women ball players. In an early scene of *The Longshots*, the head coach introduces Jasmine, the lead BWA, as the newest member of a Pop Warner football team. The team of all boys responds with an eruption of laughter as if it were a joke. Their actions suggest that a girl playing football is unrealistic. While these examples carry important aspect of gender oppression, the other forms of identity oppression, especially racism, are absent. Even more significant is the lack of BWA characters who show a racial consciousness. Failing to mention or acknowledge a Black identity contradicts Africana womanism, which prioritizes race over other identities, even gender (Hudson-Weems 1993, 2000).

In *Higher Learning*, the Black track athlete, Deja, briefly speaks of her experiences as a Black woman. Also, in *Bring It On*, the Black cheerleader Isis accuses the White cheerleaders for stealing their routine. She yells, "You didn't think a White girl thought of [those cheers]?" Although this is the film's only reference to race, the Black cheerleading squad exhibits many cultural elements. This is an aspect of Africana womanism that prioritizes an authentic cultural connection in the lives of Black women. The outward manifestation or surface structure of African culture is performed in music, dance, language, dress, and customs (Myers 2003). Much of this has been modified through African enslavement and European colonization but remains present and is found in one of the examined movies. In *Bring It On*, the Black cheerleaders infuse hip hop into their performances, use urban slang terms and syntax, and apply the African aesthetic tradition of creativity in their routine. These BWAs exhibit an African-infused style in their lives and performances, thus exhibiting an African cultural identity.

Black women determining their own reality and self-identity is important to the self-definition and self-naming elements of Africana womanism (Hudson-Weems 2000, 2–3). Although most of the young BWAs do not internalize outside definitions of them, none of them outwardly show a concern or take a conscious role in accepting, rejecting, or creating labels and names for themselves. In *The Longshots*, the uncle/coach tells the featured BWA, Jasmine, "All this I'm a girl stuff, throw it out the window. You're not a girl, you're a football player." Jasmine does not refute the gender reduction verbalized by her uncle/coach.

One of the major omissions of the BWA characters in sports films is the ability of BWAs to successfully perform both traditional and nontraditional gender roles, simultaneously. Even though Black folks have not always been free to perform the socially defined gender roles set by the dominant culture,

Black women have maintained a strong fluidity that has allowed them to contemporaneously take on various familial and social roles, as they are needed in the community. Hudson-Weems argues, "Africana women and men alike have never been so clearly defined in the Africana community and thus the roles have always been somewhat relaxed." These loose gender boundaries can be problematic if Black women do not perform socially acceptable characteristics of femininity. For example, neither Monica's mother nor her male counterparts affirm her when she is wearing her athletic clothing or cornrow hairstyle, which is convenient for playing sports. The only time Monica is complimented on her looks is when she is not carrying the image of an athlete. In one scene, during the school dance, she is wearing a form-fitting white dress and her older sister has done her makeup and hair. While at the dance her date, male best friend, and a few other men all make suggestive gestures and compliment her looks. BWAs are advised to prioritize their femininity by some and their athletic identity by others.

The inability to produce the same images of athleticism as Black men has hindered the visibility of BWAs in their respective sports and in film. Michael Messner (1996) pointed out the normalizing characteristics of an athlete. He illustrates this in a binary equation for men and women: Athleticism = Masculinity (men) / Femininity (women) = Heterosexuality. Therefore, the display of athleticism equals a display of masculinity and heterosexuality. However, the athletic abilities of females are often not as strong as males'. Therefore, showing a display of nonathleticism equals femininity. DePauw (1997) renames Messner's three socially constructed ideals to physicality, masculinity, and sexuality (421). She defines physicality as "the socially accepted view of able-bodied physical ability, or prowess, often associated with agility, aggression, and strength." Since female athletes, on average, are not as physical as male athletes, they are less than or not equal to "able-bodied," and thus rendered "disabled" (DePauw 1997, 424). DePauw explains,

> Ability is at the center of sport and physical activity. Ability, as currently socially constructed, means "able" and implies a finely tuned "able" body. On the other hand, disability, also a social construction, is often viewed in relation to ability and is, then, most often defined as "less than" ability, as not able. To be able to "see" individuals with disabilities as athletes (regardless of the impairment) requires us to redefine athleticism and our view of the body, especially the "sporting body." (DePauw 1997, 423)

The established belief that women are athletically "disabled" has resulted in the creation of gender categories in sports. In addition, the sports that are deemed less masculine, such as swimming, cheerleading, and tennis, are relegated and classified as "gender-appropriate" for women. What DePauw is suggesting in the latter part of her quote is a reframing of sports that will, in this case, find equal value in the characteristics specific to BWAs' style of play. In the movie *Love & Basketball*, the song "Light as a Rock" by Black female rapper MC Lyte accompanied a scene containing an all-Black women's high school basketball game. At the beginning of the song, Lyte says, "Do you understand the metaphor 'light as a rock'? It's explaining just how heavy the young lady is." The song coincides with BWAs' ability to display both masculine and feminine stereotypical traits, two things that are not usually associated with each other. BWAs have displayed exceptional physical strength in their respective sports. But they have also shown that their use of strength does not come at the expense of their ability to finesse, float, and move with fluidity. This provides BWAs with a different style of play than their male counterparts.

Another glaring void in the overall body of films featuring BWA characters is the absence of sisterhood. The Africana womanist carries a genuine commitment to sisterhood between herself and other Black women (Hudson-Weems 2000). Hudson-Weems describes genuine sisterhood as "an asexual relationship between women who confide in each other and willingly share their true feelings, their fears, their hopes, and their dreams" (Hudson-Weems 2000, 65). But the BWAs in the studied films do not show or develop a strong bond with other Black women. More so, they illustrate heated moments of friction with other Black sisters. Monica, in *Love & Basketball*, has conflicts with various Black women at various stages of her life, and these negative relationships dominate the portrayal of sisterhood within the movie. For example, she holds contempt for a high school classmate. In college, she has a battle for the starting position on her basketball team with a BWA teammate that turns personal. Lastly, she looks at her love interest's fiancé as competition. In other movies, scenes between BWAs are simply don't exist. *Juwanna Mann* has several bonding scenes between a BWA and a male who briefly poses as a BWA, but this is not an example of an authentic sisterhood. The failure to incorporate a genuine sisterhood into the BWA characters adds to the inauthenticity of them as Africana womanist athletes.

BLACK MALE COMPATIBILITY

Love & Basketball shows the struggle to develop and sustain a strong relationship between the two main characters, Monica and Quincy (Q). This relationship shows Monica's compatibility with a Black man that is equally supportive and reciprocal. Male compatibility is important as an Africana womanist element because neither Black men nor Black women can afford to disregard or dismiss the other. This would be the demise of the race. As a teenager, Monica shows a supportive companionship with Quincy. But as basketball became more demanding, she fails to support her male partner during his weakest moment. When questioned about her priorities regarding her relationship and her sport she replies, "I'm a ball player." Her goal of being an excellent player is more important than being in a successful relationship with Quincy.

Struggling and navigating through life in a way that is in concert with males allows for a joint and complete approach toward liberation. Monica is outdone by another BWA character, Deja, in *Higher Learning*. Deja, a BWA, has a complex supportive nature toward her male mate and fellow athlete. In an interaction on the field, she articulates how she, as a BWA, deals with racism. She asserts,

> Oh so you think I got it easy? You know the girls that I stay with? Every single time something comes up missing, who do you think they look at? Who you think they look at? I feel like fighting. I feel like beating people up. It's a waste of time. Instead I fight with this. And I'm getting mine. But you got to stop doing this [fighting others] all the time and start doing this [looking at within]. And quit worrying about what people think.

Although Deja does not acknowledge the racist targeting experienced by her male partner and Black men in general, she shows sympathy toward his frustration. Deja's solidarity with her male partner in the Black struggle is a characteristic of an Africana woman. Hudson-Weems argues, "Since Africana men have never had the same institutionalized power to oppress as have White men, family pride and solidarity are embraced warmly from the Africana woman's perspective" (2000, 7). In other words, even though patriarchy may give some privileges to Black men, their race holds them from receiving the level of benefits that White males have. After all, Black women or Black men are not each other's enemy; the enemy is the larger oppressive force of White supremacy that degrades Black women, children, and men (Hudson-Weems 2000, 25). Both Monica and Deja have illustrated a complementarity with their Black men. When asked about dating Spanish or Italian men, she replies, "They're just not my type I guess." Monica maintains her preference for Black men even when living abroad and not having access to many of them.

MONICA: AN AFRICANA WOMANIST ATHLETE IN *LOVE & BASKETBALL*

The BWA character that best models an Africana womanist is Monica from the film *Love & Basketball*. This can be attributed to the director Gina

Prince-Bythewood who is a Black woman and former college athlete. Prince-Bythewood addresses the multilayered struggles facing a BWA. Monica illustrates a combination of several Africana womanist characteristics and qualities.

One important quality is that Monica is family centered, which is a critical part of Africana womanism (Hudson-Weems 2000). Monica seems committed to building a family with her love interest. However, she is not constrained by traditional Western female roles. This is an example of the flexible role-playing ability of Africana women. Unfortunately, Monica fails to see value in the dissimilar form of family centeredness held by her mother. She describes her feelings by saying, "what is ridiculous is being a caterer so your husband can feel like a man knowing his woman is home cooking and ironing his drawers." Monica clearly views her mother's domestic role as a home wife and mother as degrading. Contrastingly, Africana womanist hold a strong belief in womanhood, motherhood, and partnership as a sacred and necessary position in society (Hudson-Weems 2000, 11). Monica's mother has maintained a strong family core by prioritizing family by adapting the space of her individual development. But Monica does not recognize the importance of domestic roles in family maintenance. Monica does, however, illustrate the Africana womanist adaptability by traveling to different schools, cities, countries, teams, and jobs. At each place she finds a way to success-fully adapt. In school and in the working world she initially struggles. But after she adapts, she eventually becomes successful.

When Monica becomes a mother herself, her family role looks different than her mother's. In the final scene, she is seen as the working parent and spouse, while her husband sits holding their child and literally cheering her in support from the sidelines. Monica's ability to be both a financial contributor and a mother illustrates her role flexibility. Monica is the only BWA character in the films examined that is or becomes a mother. This is important because Africana womanism calls for a commitment to motherhood, nurturing, pro-viding, and protecting in a way that is not exploited. Hudson-Weems notes, "the Africana woman is less inclined to focus primarily on herself and her career at the expense of the family and its needs" (Hudson-Weems 2000, 60). Eventually, Monica is shown as a working mother in a short and final scene, thus displaying her mothering and family-centered image.

CONCLUSION

The history of Black women in the United States is one that is occupied by racism and sexism that intersect to create unique forms of invisibility, objectification, and stereotyping. They have been historically oppressed by structural, cultural, legal, and social practices. Sports and film are both institutions that contribute to the lack and inauthenticity of BWA images. In saying that, there are still positive attributes that can be extracted from the characterization of BWAs, especially in the movie *Love & Basketball*. Other films with BWAs very rarely exhibit a struggle against racism or a cultural consciousness.

The disgracefully low number of movies that feature BWA characters is indicative of the intersectional oppression or more specifically race-gender double jeopardy shared by BWAs inside and outside of sports and film. Many of the movies are not written, directed, or produced by BWAs, nor Black people. We not only need more BWA characters in film but also culturally affirming and liberating portrayals of true Africana womanism. One of the major priorities of Africana womanists is wholeness or completeness, which films on BWAs have lacked (Hudson-Weems 2000, 69). Strategies for creating holistic and culturally appropriate BWA characters that do not perpetuate negative stereotypes must be employed by film writers and directors. Srividya Ramasubramanian encourages similar strategies that involve countering tactics (2007). Counterstereotype and counteroppressive initiatives help offset the lack of visibility and damaging portrayals of BWA characters.

BIBLIOGRAPHY

Ahmed, F. S. 2004. "Title IX of the 1972 Education Amendments." *Georgetown Journal of Gender and the Law* 5: 361–75.

Asante, M. K. 1987. *The Afrocentric Idea.* Philadelphia: Temple Press.

Banks-Wallace, J. 2000. "Womanist Ways of Knowing: Theoretical Considerations for Research with African American Women." *Advances in Nursing Science* 22(3): 33–45.

Bonilla-Silva, E. 2003. *Racism without Racists: Color-Blind Racism and the Persistence of Racial Inequality in the United States.* Lanham, MD: Rowman & Littlefield.

Collins, P. H. 1996. "What's in a Name? Womanism, Black Feminism, and Beyond." *The Black Scholar* 26(1): 9–17.

Crenshaw, K. 1991. "Mapping the Margins: Intersectionality, Identity Politics, and Violence against Women of Color." *Stanford Law Review* 43(6): 1241–99.

DePauw, K. P. 1997. The (In)Visibility of DisAbility: Cultural Contexts and 'Sporting Bodies.' *Quest* 49(4): 416–30.

Ferguson, J. Y. 2015. *Anna Julia Cooper: A Quintessential Leader.* PhD dissertation, Antioch University, Keene, NH.

Fryberg, S. A., and S. S. Townsend. 2008. "The Psychology of Invisibility." In *Commemorating Brown: The Social Psychology of Racism and Discrimination,* edited by G. Adams, M. Biernat, N. R. Branscombe, C. S. Crandall, & L. S. Wrightsman. Washington, DC: American Psychological Association.

Griffin, R. A. 2012. "I AM an Angry Black Woman: Black Feminist Autoethnography, Voice, and Resistance." *Women's Studies in Communication* 35(2): 138–57.

Grindstaff, L., and E. West. 2006. "Cheerleading and the Gendered Politics of Sport." *Social Problems* 53(4): 500–18.

Hall, R. L. 2001. "Shaking the Foundation: Women of Color in Sport." *Sport Psychologist* 15(4): 386–400.

Holland, J. W. 2002. *Black Recreation: A Historical Perspective.* Lanham, MD: Rowman & Littlefield.

Hooks, B. 2004. *We Real Cool: Black Men and Masculinity.* New York: Routledge.

Hudson-Weems, C. 1993. *Africana Womanism: Reclaiming Ourselves.* Troy, MI: Bedford.

———. 1997. "Africana Womanism and the Critical Need for Africana Theory and Thought." *Western Journal of Black Studies* 21(2): 79.

———. 2000. "Africana Womanism: An Overview." In *Out of the Revolution: The Development of Africana Studies,* edited by D. P. Aldridge and C. Young, 205–17. Lanham, MD: Lexington Books.

Karenga, T., and C. Tembo. 2012. "Kawaida Womanism: African Ways of Being Woman in the World." *Western Journal of Black Studies* 36(1): 33.

King, D. K. 1988. "Multiple Jeopardy, Multiple Consciousness: The Context of a Black Feminist Ideology." *Signs* 14(1): 42–72.

Lansbury, J. H. 2014. *A Spectacular Leap: Black Women Athletes in Twentieth-Century America.* Fayetteville: University of Arkansas Press.

Lewis, T. 2010. *Ballers of the New School: Race and Sports in America.* Chicago: Third World Press.

Messner, M. A. 1996. "Studying Up on Sex." *Sociology of Sport Journal* 13: 221–37.

Muhammad, G. E., and S. A. McArthur. 2015. "'Styled by Their Perceptions': Black Adolescent Girls Interpret Representations of Black Females in Popular Culture." *Multicultural Perspectives* 17(3): 133–40.

Myers, L. J. 2003. "The Deep Structure of Culture: The Relevance of Traditional African Culture in Contemporary Life." In *The Afrocentric Paradigm,* edited by A. Mazama, 121–30. Trenton, NJ: African World Press.

Omolade, B. 1995. "Hearts of Darkness." In *Words of Fire: An Anthology of African-American Feminist Thought,* edited by B. Guy-Sheftall, 362–78. New York: New Press.

Pearson, D. W. 2001. "The Depiction and Characterization of Women in Sport Films." *Women in Sport and Physical Activity Journal* 10(1): 103.

Ramasubramanian, S. 2007. "Media-Based Strategies to Reduce Racial Stereotypes Activated by News Stories." *Journalism and Mass Communication Quarterly* 84(2): 249–64.

Rhoden, W. 2004. *Forty Million Dollar Slaves.* New York: Random House.

Royster, J. J. 2000. *Traces of a Stream: Literacy and Social Change among African American Women.* Pittsburgh: University of Pittsburgh Press.

Sesko, A. K. 2011. *(In)visibility of Black Women: Drawing Attention to Individuality.* PhD dissertation, University of Kansas.

Sesko, A. K., and M. Biernat. 2010. "Prototypes of Race and Gender: The Invisibility of Black Women." *Journal of Experimental Social Psychology* 46(2): 356–60.

Sidanius, J., and R. C. Veniegas. 2000. Gender and Race Discrimination: The Interactive Nature of Disadvantage. In *Reducing Prejudice and Discrimination,* edited by S. Oskamp, 47–69. Mahwah, NJ: Lawrence Erlbaum.

Thomas, A. J. 2004. "Toward the Development of the Stereotypic Roles for Black Women Scale." *Journal of Black Psychology* 30(3): 426–42.

Thompson, A. 2013. "Where Are the Black Women in Hollywood?" *USA Today,* December 17. http://www.usatoday.com/story/life/people/2013/12/17/hollywood-turns-a-blind-eye-to-black-women-in-film-tv/3443751/.

Vertinsky, P., and G. Captain. 1998. "More Myth Than History: American Culture and Representations of the Black Female's Athletic Ability." *Journal of Sport History* 23(5): 532–61.

Walker, A. 1983. *In Search of Our Mothers' Gardens.* San Diego: Harcourt.

Wallace, M. 2003. "The Good Lynching and The Birth of a Nation: Discourses and Aesthetics of Jim Crow." *Cinema Journal* 43(1): 85–104.

West, C. M. 1995. "Mammy, Sapphire, and Jezebel: Historical Images of Black Women and Their Implications for Psychotherapy." *Psychotherapy: Theory, Research, Practice, Training* 32(3): 458.

Chapter 5

Pan-African Belize

A Case for Praxis

Devon Lee

Pan-Africanism embodies the shared connection between Black people collectively reaching toward equality, while affirming notions of identity *as* African or a descendant of Africa. Kurt Young's *Case for a Belizean Pan-Africanism*, which defines representations of Pan-Africanism as "fusing of affirmations of African identity with libratory efforts at the level of the masses," details representations of Pan-Africanism from the emergence of maroon societies to Black Nationalism (Young, 2009, 7). This paper locates Belizean Pan-Africanism as a twentieth-century phenomenon rooted in the tenets of self-knowledge and self-determination inspired by Garveyism and its contemporary legacies. Marcus Garvey and others recognized knowledge of self and the use of that knowledge to forge equity as the quintessential expression of Pan-Africanism. In that sense, Black people have historically utilized Pan-Africanism as an ideological tool weaponized for liberation. This project attempts to illustrate the historical development of Pan-Africanism as praxis in Belize.[1]

Past research on Pan-Africanism in Belize has typically focused on Garveyism and Black Nationalism separately, or as the former influencing the latter. O. Nigel Bolland illustrates how the influence of the United Negro Improvement Association (UNIA) mobilized (primarily Black) Belizeans in an anti-colonial struggle (Bolland 2003). Bolland, Tom Barry, and Dylon Vernon also demonstrate how members of Pan-African groups held positions of influence in Belize's labor and national movements (Bolland 2003; Barry and Vernon 1995). Peter Ashdown and United Black Association for Development (UBAD) founder Evan X Hyde collectively make the connection between Garveyism and (Evan X Hyde) Black Power in noting the origin of UBAD and their attempted infiltration of the UNIA (Ashdown 1990; Hyde 1995). However, none of the aforementioned discusses the legacy of Garveyism and its historical sociopolitical evolution as praxis.

The purpose of this project is to show the historical development of Pan-Africanism in Belize as a process that evolved alongside political necessity. This process merged the revolutionary ideas of Marcus Garvey into revolutionary practice that forever changed the political landscape of Belize to be increasingly more responsive to the needs of the masses. Pan-Africanism in Belize has been the weaponization of intellectual discourse as praxis for political liberation through the historical development of a national identity.

TRANSNATIONAL LINKAGES BETWEEN GARVEYISM AND BLACK POWER IN BELIZE

Marcus Garvey, author of *Negro World* and founder of Harlem-based UNIA, visited Belize twice on a tour of Central America between 1910 and 1912, in July 1921, and finally in February of 1929 (Ashdown 1990). The *Negro World* newspaper was banned in Belize under the "Defense of the Colony" regulation in January 1919 (Martin 1983: 303) due to its anti-colonial rhetoric and agency that sought "the whole Negro race will be elevated to a position of world recognition" (Garvey 2014:92). On July 8, 1919, returning World War I veterans serving the British Empire disembarked off the shore of Belize City from the British ship, *Veronj,* to find themselves treated like second-class citizens (Ashdown 1989; Bolland 2003). The servicemen, unable to partake in the gainful employment promised to them as a reward for their service, and barred from joining the all-white golf club and barred, along with ministerial positions, prompted a large-scale riot on July 22 (Ashdown 1989; Dylan and Vernon 1986). On July 22, returning soldiers, along with many of the unemployed, responded to racism while serving abroad and at home through street revolts beginning on July 22 (Ashdown 1990; Martin 1976; Shoeman 2000). Governor Eyre Hutson attributed the *Negro World* newspaper, published through Marcus Garvey's Harlem-based UNIA as a cause for unrest, noting its increase of circulation, smuggled through Guatemala and Mexico, after being banned earlier that year (Ashdown 1990; Martin 1976, Martin 1983). Following the 1919 revolt, UNIA was later chartered in Belize City in March of 1920 as a result of attempted repression and further served as a catalyst for formalized Black political organization in Belize (Martin 1976: 89). In an April 29, 1920, speech to the Philadelphia Academy of Music, Garvey held British Honduras UNIA to high esteem by saying,

> Those of you who have been reading *The Negro World* will remember that about six months ago the government of British Honduras, through its legislature, voted to suppress *The Negro World* to prevent it from entering into British Honduras, where it had a circulation of 500 copies weekly. We had not yet

organized a branch of the U.N.I.A., but the moment that the government closed down the Negro World the Negro people in British Honduras—In the city of Belize—organized a branch of UNIA. (Young 2009, 2)

Organization of the UNIA in Belize was the first politically and racially conscious organization to be organized on a mass scale that engaged in global discourse. More importantly, it reflects a process whereby self-knowledge: an awareness of social position through the *Negro World* which was followed by self-determination: collective agency that reflected interests that transcended class boundaries.

Pan-Africanism: The Link between the Labor and National Movements

C. H. Grant describes Belizean Pan-Africanism as a simultaneous labor and political movement that cut across class divisions (2008). Grant declares:

> The leaders of several Black middle class groups took advantage of the situation to exert pressure upon the colonial system not only in their own interests but also on behalf of the disadvantaged and oppressed. This marked a new phase of political evolution in the region in that it created a dichotomy by which economic power remained in the hands of a white managerial class and politics was opened to a variety of black elements. (Grant 2008, 67)

Samuel Haynes, the founder of UNIA British Honduras (colonial Belize) and writer of the Belizean national anthem, once said, Garvey "gave something to the Negro which neither time, nor place can retrieve" as he "brought the Negro people of the world into one family through the propagation of a program which gave birth to an international comity" (Ashdown 1990: 11). Here, Haynes acknowledged that mass appeal of Pan-Africanism through Marcus Garvey's ideas as a force of solidarity. Haynes adds to this in saying "Garvey sold the Negro to himself" (Martin 1976: 18). Through these collective statements, self-knowledge and self-determination are equivalent to the understanding of oppression of a distinct racial group and agency to use that understanding to forge a more dignified existence. Self-ownership, as referred to by Haynes, is then an anti-domination perspective that allows people to define their own terms of existence; rather than be subjected to a predetermined social position.

The thought evoked in Garveyism psychologically empowered Blacks to withstand social and political domination and be proprietors of their own destiny. Garvey once said, "The white man taught that the best of the world was intended for him, and we now teach that all the beauties of creation are the Black man's, and he is heir to all that God has given man" (Martin 1976: 89).

Garveyism provided the springboard for the labor movement by creating a
lens for Blacks to see their exploitation and inspire change. This naturally led
to the anti-colonial/national movement in Belize and later served as a framework for post-colonial projects (Ashdown 1990, Bolland 2003, Shoeman
2000, Young 2009). O. Nigel Bolland references "Calvert Staine, who was a
Vice President of Belize UNIA and later Chairman of the Belize Town Board
and a member of the Legislative Council" (Bolland 2003). Staine's role as
a Garveyite and politician represents the role that Garveyism had in shaping
Belizean politics. The Marcus Garvey historian Tony Martin refers to the
founder of Belize UNIA and columnist of *The Negro World*, Samuel Haynes,
in his conclusion that Garvey demonstrated that Black people could be organized and were eager to support sincere Black leadership (Martin 1976: 58).

Garveyite and *Belize Independent* columnist LD Kemp, along with Gar-
veyite labor organizer Antonio Soberanis cowrote *The Third Side of the
Anglo-Guatemalan Dispute over Belize or British Honduras* (Soberanis and
Kemp 1949). In this pamphlet, the writers protest against the imperial impo-
sitions of Britain and Guatemala. Kemp also wrote a column in the "Belize
Independent," *The Garvey Eye*, which functioned as a resource for consciousness (self-knowledge) (McPherson 2007; Bolland 2003). This alongside and
Soberanis' agency as a key organizer in the labor movement (self-determination) demonstrate interlocking efforts toward the objective of liberation
(Grant 2008, Shoeman 2000). The linkage between Garveyism, Belizean
labor, and political representation is one that cannot easily be denied. Labor
unions were both preceded and framed by UNIA. From the cartoons calling
Blacks to vote and make a stand to not be denied, to poems and publications
advocating for self-determination, Garveyism empowered Blacks to organize
for economic uplift (Martin 1976: 217–219; Hill 2006; Garvey 2014).

Labor organization in Belize began through activism, "When a group
calling itself the 'Unemployed Brigade' marched through Belize Town on
14 February 1934, it started a broad movement that had a lasting effect on
Belizean politics" (Bolland, 2003). The labor movement in Belize began
with the Unemployed Brigade demand for a cash dole (Bolland 2003). This
found limited success, leaving the unemployed restless (Bolland, 2003).
Their unrest was seen as ineffective and the Unemployed Brigade was then
uprooted through the leadership of Antonio Soberanis of the Laborers Unemployed Association's (LUA) and their demand for livable wages (Merill,
1993). LUA's flag flew the green, black, and red of Garvey's UNIA, while
the organization was peopled by members of Belize's UNIA (Bolland, 2003).
Their organization was met with colonial hostility (Bolland 2003: 169). Laws
banning criticism of the colonial government were enacted in 1935, followed
by Soberanis being jailed for sedition and LUA disintegrating (Barry and
Dylan 1995: 92).

In 1939, former LUA activists became leaders in the Native First movement, which won seats on the Belize Town Council (Barry and Dylan 1995).
In 1941, Soberanis created the British Honduras Workers Trade Union
(BHWTU) because, as he said: "trade unionism is ... the only medium by
which the working class can get a square deal" (Shoeman 2000: 174). In
1941, there were still trade union and master-servant ordinances that made
strike or any form of a "breach of contract" illegal (Shoeman 2000). Through
collective bargaining, the Trade Union Ordinance was lifted in 1941, along
with the Masters and Servants Ordinance of 1883 and Fraudulent Labour-
ers Ordinance of 1922 being lifted in 1943 (Bolland 2003 and Grant 2008).
Prior to 1943, poor wages created living conditions that were similar to the
working conditions of nineteenth-century slavery (Shoeman 2000, 168).
Direct action by Soberanis and others then worked to amend that sense of
economic oppression by empowering the working class generally and Blacks
specifically.

By 1947, the General Workers Union (GWU) had drawn so much support
that, in 1947, it was able to win all elected seats in Stann Creek, thereby setting a precedent as the first political organization in Belize (Shoeman 2000:
175). In this same year, George Price was an elected member of the Belize
Town Council on the Native First ticket, the same group that grew out of
the disintegration of LUA. The mobilization of UNIA (circa 1920s) created
the organizational background for the formation of the GWU (circa 1940s)
and later the People's United Party (PUP) in the 1950s (Bolland 2003, 189).
The success of the GWU followed by the British Government's decision to
devalue the Belizean dollar in 1949 caused the focus of active Belizeans to
shift emphasis from labor organization to political organization (Grant 2008;
Shoeman 2000; Bolland 2003). Devaluation undermined all previous labor
organizing efforts by imposing colonial control over the value of labor and
ultimately devaluing workers.

George Price, who was the leader of the PUP, Premier of Belize in 1950,
the first prime minister in 1981, and a proponent of national unity, said on
January 6, 1950:

National unity! That is the keynote of this phase of our history. This unity is
welding our people into a united, solid front. From the districts come assurances
of support in our fight against devaluation .... We must continue this movement
towards national unity. We must unite and organize ourselves in strong labour
unions, strong credit unions, cooperatives, to present a solid front against the
possible invasion of any exploiting capital. (Shoeman 2000: 184)

This quote signifies the culmination of Garveyite efforts that promoted
unity alongside anti-colonial sentiment. Central to Price's argument was the

coming together against economic exploitation. However, this perspective usurped the centrality of race imbedded within the Garveyism. Removing the racial critique of colonial exploitation, also removed the racial experience of Black Belizeans. This adaptive shift was inevitably important in maintaining support from US conglomerates like the United Fruit Company as well as the international church community (Moberg 1997; Hyde 1995). However, it also created an avenue for continued ethnic antagonism as self-governance evolved.

The PUP, the first political party of Belize, adopted the Westminster model of government. The Westminster model of government also reaffirmed the British system of domination that created governance which ignored conflict that was not explicitly "political" (Nowottney 2007). The political model assumes the popular vote, in and of itself, is representative of people notwithstanding the fact that the leaders of the political parties are not elected by the people, but by the party. This model was not adapted to the social context of Belize, and, as such, created similar conditions that were present in the colonial system prior to the self-governing transition into independence set forth in 1964. In *Colonialism and Resistance in Belize: Essays in Historical Sociology*, O. Nigel Bolland adds to this by observing, "political party affiliation constitutes an identity that often cross-cuts rather than reinforces ethnic identity because party politics is not organized along ethnic lines" (2003). Simply, the political elite became the decision makers on behalf of the masses, reestablishing a colonial process for governance.

BLACK POWER/BLACK NATIONALISM
REPACKAGED AND TRANSPORTED TO BELIZE

On November 13, 1966, Stokely Carmichael spoke about Black Power at Dartmouth College in New Hampshire. In this speech, Carmichael recognized Black Power as the definition of self and organization by which Blacks needed to subvert white supremacist practices and frameworks; Carmichael said,

> Our concern for Black Power addresses itself directly to this problem. The necessity to reclaim our history and identity from the cultural terrorism and self-justifying white guilt. To this we move for the right to create our own terms through which to define ourselves and our relationship to the society; and to have these terms recognized.

As the centerpiece of his speech, this quote notes white supremacy as cultural terrorism and Black Power as the subversive stand that Black folks must take by defining themselves and where they fit in society. In this speech, Carmichael packaged self-knowledge as a self-created group consciousness of political position, and self-determination as agency designed to fit the needs of the people. Carmichael may not have borrowed the words, but he borrowed the framework of Pan-Africanist Garveyism. On the night that Carmichael spoke to the audience of Dartmouth, Evan (X) Hyde was in the audience. Although he was not a participant of the Black Power Movement at the time, Hyde later adopted Black Nationalism and later Pan-Africanism from Carmichael (Hyde 1995).

On June 30, 1968, Evan X Hyde returned to Belize after attending Dartmouth College in New Hampshire, United States (Hyde 1995). Hyde began his influence in Belize with the sole ambition to bring Black Power to Belize "to unite the Black people of Southeast Asia, Latin America, the United States and Afro Honduras ... . To fight against the white imperialists of America, Russia and Great Britain" (Hyde 1995: 38). This influence began at the height of the Black Power Movement in 1968. Hyde's Black nationalism adopted the multicultural outlook that represents the Belizean collective, which, at surface value, is in line with the political design of the PUP. However, the discerning factor between the two was Hyde's recognition of white supremacy as creating an oppressive element for (primarily) Black (and Mayan) Belizeans. Hyde's influence was made through organizing UBAD and publishing the [still running] *Amandala* newspaper (Hyde 1995). The *Amandala* was the extension of UBAD and gave voice to Black and Indigenous history and culture, while extending revolutionary ideas as a tool for empowerment. In an email responding to my asking the purpose of *Amandala* on May 16, 2012, Evan X Hyde wrote that the newspaper was "the voice of UBAD which would allow me to write with freedom"; this freedom was framed by the notion of development that sought to uplift the collectively oppressed.

UBAD consequently came as a source of education and empowerment that developed into racial discourse and political critique (Hyde 1995). Hyde and the supporters of UBAD felt that Blacks were not in the position to know about themselves and appreciate their history as an empowering history. Responding to disempowerment, Hyde began teaching literature at the University of Belize (Hyde 1995). This teaching post later turned into a public podium where Hyde found that political empowerment was more useful than education alone (Hyde 1995). The first issue of the *Amandala*, which went into circulation on August 13, 1969, entitled "Where We Are Coming From," introduced racial, cultural, and political discourse through its mission: "We believe a knowledge of the past, a knowledge of self and kind, will give us a mandate to revolutionize this corrupt whitewashed society in which we live." The *Amandala,* therefore, introduced discourse as an intervention to the integration of white supremacy into the workings of self-government. The newspaper, therefore, operationalized self-knowledge, while at the same time adapting Black Power to the cultural makeup of Belize.

POLITICAL OPPOSITION TO BLACK POWER

The leaders of the anti-colonial movement saw the stance of UBAD as "defiance" and undermining the efforts of the nationalist movement. In an article entitled "67/78 Decade of Changes Chapter 1 From Fists to Guns" printed on April 7, 1978, Evan X Hyde notes that the UBAD riot of 1972 drew more protesters than its Garveyite predecessor in 1919, implicitly acknowledging its relevant and supported stance against neocolonial oppression (Hyde 1978). As UBAD stood against the PUP's lack of representative democracy, the PUP saw UBAD as an impediment to the national movement and a threat to national independence.

Religious and economic power-brokers found the condemnation of white supremacy threatening and politicians promoting national unity found UBAD divisive (Hyde, 1995). As such, the PUP (in particular) saw Black Power as something that needed to be put down. In an unpublished reflection piece held at the Heritage Library in Belmopan, Belize, UBAD cofounder Ishmail Shabazz sarcastically explained expectations in saying, "We must not teach Black consciousness because this is racism. Most of all we were supposed to preach the love of a God who looks like himself both the PUP and NIP came together to condemn UBAD" (LVF Political Groups [2] p.2). Politicians found the rhetoric and purpose of UBAD as threatening because if accepted as appealing to the masses, the message would inherently undermine the economic concessions and clientelism that empowered government. In an effort to destroy UBAD, PUP-affiliated police officers were deployed at UBAD breakfasts; spies at meetings and charges of seditions were filed in response to government officials being accused of "playing politics" (Hyde 1995: 63). These were also the tactics used against labor and political organizers under the colonial system.

Ishmail Shabazz notes that the result of the conflict was awareness in saying, "This attack by the political parties only help to raise the consciousness of the people" (Shabazz 1991: 2). UBAD supporters found the PUP government to be "a stooge for white power and neocolonialism" (Hyde 1995: 21). The national project directed by the political leaders formed a type of neocolonialism that allowed "90 percent of Belize's privately owned land, including most of the nation's prime agricultural areas and tourists facilities" to be owned primarily by American citizens and other foreigners in the late 80s (Merill et. al. 1993: 204). To this regard, the economic market was dominated by US industry and an economic situation that removed the ability of Belizean citizens to own land and grow industry through self-determination. In an *Amandala* article published On April 14, 1978, an *Amandala* article entitled "From Pine Resin to Black Gold," Hyde demonstrates that the profit of resin has shifted toward the exploration of oil and has thereby created a situation whereby "our legislators and police have become target for big money offers to turn their heads the other way." In an *Amandala* editorial entitled "The Merchant of Venice," published on March 25, 1988, Evan X Hyde adds to this notion by suggesting that politicians model Shakespeare's Shylock and set the terms of economic relationships, rather than be subject to unreasonable loan terms.

These two articles demonstrate a neocolonial trend through the political practice of clientelism. James Robinson defines clientelism as "a political exchange: a politician (i.e., a 'patron') gives patronage in exchange for the vote or support of a 'client.' The dominant stylized fact in this body of literature is that, in clientelism, it is jobs that are exchanged for vote" (Robinson and Verdier 2013: 262). In this case, the promise of jobs has historically been used to "buy votes" as a form of patronage to reproduce power; power that has been dictated by global powers (IMF/World Bank) that ultimately position politicians to be dictators.

The Belizean government is the largest provider of middle-class jobs. This created an apathetic middle class that was not in the position to challenge sociopolitical issues. In an interview on July 5, 2010, Evan X Hyde expanded on this point:

> The electoral political system is so powerful because of the amount of jobs that are involved. You looking at thousands of jobs which an elected political party controls and I'm talking about jobs that does very little ... just a simple thing like a driver's job, a lot of jobs that change when the parties change. The struggle is so intense because there is a huge impact on an underclass of people who are often unemployed or semi-employed.

During the time of UBAD, this meant that the majority of youth and underemployed were a "nonfactor" to be considered in representative politics. The provision of jobs is then a neocolonial token that purchases silence by forcing citizens to replace subversion with apathy.

ADAPTIVE CHARACTER AND LATENT STAGE

Although UBAD was disbanded by 1975, the Pan-African ideal of Black Nationalism was relatively achieved (Hyde 2003). The consistent critique of the neocolonial condition and drive toward Black empowerment through the *Amandala*, along with critiques of the PUP, changed the way the PUP responded to the needs of the people. By 1975, the PUP brought in prominent activists associated with UBAD, including Evan X Hyde (Grant 2008, Hyde 2003). The PUP stood its ground to promote jobs and to stand against neocolonial practices [albeit, only relative to the opposing and more conservative United Democratic Party]. UNIA showed the same transition of utility and disappearance as UBAD. Once the organization served its purpose, it vanished, infiltrating problematic institutions and in practice, evolving into something that better served the needs of the masses.

The transition from Garveyism to Labor began a transition away from empowerment and into action. In this sense, the self-knowledge was used to build a capacity for agency. The colonial system responded to unrest and the generation of self-knowledge by creating new oppressive conditions, namely the banning of the *Negro World*, as well as anti-sedition laws of 1935 leading to the arrest of Antonio Soberanis. From that point, the Belizean masses were transitioning from labor organizing and into political organizing. After labor gains were achieved, the colonial system adapted to maintain oppressive conditions by devaluing the Belizean dollar. This cemented the national movement, which removed self-knowledge elements central to the Garvey influence. This created a vacuum that was later filled by the presence of UBAD and their version of Black Power. As needs changed, so did organizing principles in the form of self-knowledge and the self-determination (political organization) that followed. UBAD utilized discourse to challenge the existing political structure; effectively injecting self-knowledge lost in transition from Garveyism to the movement for national independence.

Currently, the Belizean self-knowledge aspect of Pan-Africanism imbeds itself into the consciousness of Belizeans through KREM Productions (an outgrowth of the *Amandala*), and the way in which the political system has to respond to the nation's most popular independent production company. The English translation of the Zulu word *Amandala* means "Power to the People." This is also the slogan (Power to the People) of the PUP. The determination aspect of the KREM Production is its provision of jobs and its influence on the nation's political response to meet the economic needs of the people. As a flexible intervention, the Black power aesthetic in Belize has expanded to represent the predominantly non-white collective, and most powerfully, speaks to the conditions of the most marginalized. Contemporary Pan-Africanism in Belize exhibits praxis with malleable definitions that attempt to meet the needs of the masses, expressed in what I identified as the adaptive characteristic.

Belizean Pan-Africanism has so thoroughly infiltrated the sociopolitical culture that it has become Belizean. The Belizean case is one that shows a desired future for Pan-Africanism whereby a Black issue becomes a non-white or humanitarian issue that advocates and empowers most (if not all) by imbedding self-determination and self-knowledge into a consistent and contextually flexible political discourse. In doing so, it has, however, become less distinctly Black in its political application. Simultaneously, it has also created a language and platform for corrective interventions similar to that of UBAD. This adaptive framework that operationalizes the position of the collectively oppressed as a critique of the system or organizing principle has been and continues to be the galvanizing factor for many grassroots organizations.

NOTE

1. Belize was formerly known as British Honduras during its colonization and officially adopted its current name in 1973.

BIBLIOGRAPHY

Ashdown, Peter. 1990. "Garveyism in Belize." *Society for the Preservation of Education and Research.* Belize
———. 1989. "Race Riot, Class Warfare and 'Coup d'etat: The Ex-Serviceman's Riot of July 1919." *Amandala.* April 14.
Barry, Tom and Vernon Dylan. 1995. *Inside Belize: The Essential Guide to its Politics, Economy, Society, and Environment.* Albuquerque: Resource Center Press.
Belize.com. "Current Oil Exploration in Belize." Retrieved April 20, 2011 http://www.belize.com/articles/oil-exploration-in-belize.html.
Bolland, O. Nigel. 2003. *Colonialism and Resistance in Belize: Essays in Historical Sociology.* Belize: Cubola Books.
Blumer, Herbert. 1958. "Race Prejudice as a Sense of Group Position." University of California Press. *The Pacific Sociological Review*, 1(1): 3–7.
Carmichael, Stokely. 1966. *Black Power.* Speech at Dartmouth College, New Hampshire, November 13.
———. 1971. *From Black Power to Pan-Africanism.* Whittier College, Whittier, California. March 22.
Fanon, Franz. 2004. *Wretched of the Earth.* New York: Grove Press.
Farrakhan, Louis. 1986. "15-Day Royal Princess Caribbean Tour," *Address to the Belizean People.*
Garvey, Marcus. 1987. *Marcus Garvey Life and Lessons,* edited by R.A. Hill and B. Blair. Los Angeles: University of California Press.
———. 2014. *Philosophy and Opinions of Marcus Garvey.* New Jersey: Frank Cass and Co. Ltd.
Grant, C.H. 2008. *The Making of Modern Belize: Politics, Society and British Colonialism in Central America.* New York: Columbia University Press.

Hill, Robert. 2006. *The Marcus Garvey and Universal Negro Improvement Association Papers.* Los Angeles: University of California Press.

Hyde, Evan X. 1978. "67/78 Decade of Changes Chapter 1 From Fists to Guns." *Amandala.* April 7.

———. 2010. Interviewed by author. Belize City, Belize. July 5.

———. 1995. *X Communication.* Belize City: Angulus Press.

Martin, Tony. 1976. *Race First: The Ideological and Organizational Struggles of Marcus Garvey and the Universal Negro Improvement Association.* Westport: Greenwood Press.

———. 1983. *The Marcus Garvey and Universal Negro Improvement Association Papers, Volume 2.* Edited by Tolbert, Emory and Forzek, Deborah. University of California Press: Los Angeles.

McPherson, Anne. 2007. *From Colony to Nation: Women Activists and the Gendering of Politics in Belize, 1912—1982.* Lincoln: University of Nebraska Press.

Merrill, Tim. 1992. *Belize: A Country Study.* Washington: GPO for the Library of Congress.

Merill et. al. 1993. *Guyana and Belize Country Studies.* Washington, DC: Library of Congress Press.

Nowottny, Mark. 2007. *'No Tyrants Here Linger': Understandings of Democracy in Modern Belize.* MSc dissertation, Institute for the Study of the Americas. September 7.

Robinson, James and Thiery Verdier. 2013. "The Political Economy of Clientelism." *The Scandinavian Journal of Economics* 115(2): 260–91.

Shabazz, Ishmail. 1991. Unpublished Manuscript, "UBAD Experience and Legacy." Herritage Library LVF Political Groups [2] p.2. Publication date unknown.

Shoeman, Assad. 2000. *Thirteen Chapters of a History of Belize.* Belize: Angelus Press.

Soberanis, Antonio and Kemp, Luke D. 1949. *The Third Side of the Anglo-Guatemalan Dispute Over Belize or British Honduras.* Belize: Open Forum.

Ture, Kwame and Charles Hamilton. 1992. *Black Power.* New York: Vantage Books.

Vernon, Lawrence. *A History of Political Parties in Belize 1950—81.* Unpublished text (accessed September 20, 2011).

Young, Kurt B. 2009. "The Case for a Belizean Pan-Africanism." *The Journal of Pan African Studies* 2(9).

Chapter 6

Insights Regarding Black-White Economic Inequality from Stratification Economics

James B. Stewart

This chapter uses concepts from the emerging subfield of Stratification Economics to explore the causes of persisting Black-White economic inequality in the US. Stratification Economics (SE) that has the potential to significantly advance our understanding regarding the role of economic forces in intensifying or mitigating conflicts between "racial" groups. In addition, SE facilitates an understanding of the extent to which economic institutions are efficiently organized and operated while simultaneously accommodating sustained patterns of racial stratification.

The importance of the "group" within various aspects of African American culture is well established. The collective economic interests among African Americans originate in the communal traditions of traditional African societies. The pursuit of potential gains from collective action has been reinforced by the common patterns of oppression experienced by individuals during different historical periods from the era of slavery until the present. Conversely, the collective economic interests of whites derive from the ideology of white racial superiority and wide access to economic rents generated at the expense of African Americans and other nonwhite groups.

From the perspective of SE racial identity can be thought of as a type of individual and group property that has both income and wealth-generating characteristics. Race is conceptualized as a produced form of personal identity whose supply and demand is responsive to changes in production costs and budget constraints. However, individual choice does not guarantee social recognition or acceptance. Others' ascriptions of racial identity may differ from that desired by an individual and those ascriptions can influence economic opportunities and outcomes.

The treatment of race and racial identity in SE differs markedly from what is found in other economic approaches. Neoclassical economists typically think of social identities as characteristics of an individual that are not economically productive, but which may have economic consequences. As a result, the scrutiny of race is relegated to a secondary status relative to other forces deemed to be more important for economic decision-making. As an illustration, economist Kenneth Arrow, a Nobel laureate, captures the essence of the standard neoclassical approach to examining race as follows:

> The black steel worker may be thought of as producing blackness as well as steel, both evaluated in the market. We are singling out the former as a special subject for analysis because somehow we think it is appropriate for the steel industry to produce steel and not for it to produce a black or white work force. (Arrow 1974, 4)

The decentering of race in traditional economic analysis has shaped how neoclassical economists approach the study of racial inequality. The neoclassical approach is encapsulated into what can be characterized as the subfield of the "economics of discrimination." This subfield has its origins in the notion of a "taste for discrimination," introduced by another Nobel economic laureate, Gary Becker.

Becker's well-known "taste" or preference theory of discrimination asked a rather simple question: if there is a subset of individuals within society who regard economic association with other racially distinct individuals as an economic bad, will these tastes for discrimination have a sustained impact on economic outcomes? The individuals with a preference for discrimination may be consumers, employers, or employees. Becker argued that although this form of bigotry may produce a certain degree of segregation, such preferences will not produce sustained inter-racial differences in wages, employment, or occupational attainment when the general conditions for a competitive economy are met. The key conclusion flowing from Becker's model is that the competitive forces of the market will undermine the economic impact of irrational preferences. For Becker, bigotry is an irrational preference since it is exogenously given and can only be maintained at a prohibitive cost to the employer, employee, or consumer because nondiscriminating owners of capital will choose profits over racism in making resource allocation decisions. Presumably, discriminating owners will either be forced out of business or modify their behavior to be competitive, although the time period over which such market adjustments could be expected to occur is never formally specified.

There are at least two major issues that raise serious questions about the operational usefulness of the neoclassical approach for interpreting the forces that produce racial economic inequality in the real world and offering viable recommendations for reducing such inequality. The first issue is the extent to which market imperfections limit the type of anti-discriminatory responses predicted by the competitive model. Many studies continue to find evidence of labor market discrimination and discrimination in other economic activities including human capital investment options and choice of residence. In response SE analysts ask the following questions: (1) Does the persistence of discrimination simply imply that markets are not sufficiently competitive to achieve the predicted outcome? (2) If noncompetitive markets are the norm in the United States have discriminating agents developed ways to adapt institutions to accommodate discriminatory preferences such that losses in efficiency are minimized? (3) Have discriminating agents found strategies to shift the burden of economic losses resulting from discriminatory practices onto the victims? (4) If structural adaptations are possible that allow relatively costless discrimination to operate (from the vantage point of discriminators) do members of a dominant group have any incentive to seek information about the social costs of discrimination and racial stratification or undertake actions to mitigate them? Mason (1999, 1995), Williams (1991), and Darity and Williams (1985) have demonstrated convincingly that competition is not only consistent with discrimination, but competition creates material incentives to persistently reproduce discriminatory behavior.

A second issue treated inadequately in the neoclassical paradigm is the presumed irrationality of so-called "tastes for discrimination." Becker did not treat the origin of a taste for discrimination, bigotry, as an economic question. However, when racial identity is conceptualized in economic terms, the presumed power of competitive markets to punish decisions based solely on racial preferences is diminished considerably. Whites who benefit directly or indirectly from discrimination that victimizes other groups have few incentives to oppose systems of racial domination and, in fact, can easily become avid supporters. Darity and Williams (1985, 259–60) argue, for example, that "workers can ... concentrate and consolidate, particularly by ethnicity or race." This is accomplished, Darity and Williams argue, "via control of training, evaluation, information, and the definition of jobs," that allows "winners in early rounds of labor market competition ... [to] insulate themselves from the most recent recruits to the wage labor force."

SE proponents argue that the norms of collective racial identity emerge as a critical mass of persons engaged in own-group altruism and other-group antagonism. Once a sufficiently large number of persons begin to engage in racialized behavior, there are increasing economic incentives for all persons to engage in racialized behavior. Racialized behavior spreads throughout society because individuals observe that own-group altruism and other-group antagonism is an income-increasing strategy relative to individualist behavior where neither altruism nor antagonism is involved in exchange with other persons. Moreover, each agent's payoff to racialized behavior increases with the mean wealth of the agent's group. Income and wealth inequality increase the incentives for racialized behavior.

The aggregate constellation of behaviors and values of individuals who actively identify with a particular racial classification constitutes what can be described as collective racial identity. The existence of this type of quasi-kinship-based affiliation among individuals emerges from basic human instincts that are primordial in nature. However, it is social institutions that codify definitions of, and the boundaries between, racial groups. In the United States, the record of governmental specification of rules of racial classification associated with peoples of African descent is well known. Such classifications were established both through legislation and court decisions. The categories mulatto, quadroon, and octoroon were purported to designate an individual's degree of African ancestry. These were given official status not only to distinguish patterns of descent, but also to assign differential opportunities.

Collective racial identity, as understood by SE researchers, is not easily categorized using traditional economic terminology. Collective racial identity has some characteristics similar to what economists term "externalities," that is, output created by other productive activities. This collective identity has a positive value for those who identify with it or benefit unconsciously from its existence, but can have negative effects on those who identify with a different racial/cultural identity. However, collective racial identity also has dimensions that are like "public goods," which are nonexcludable and nonrival in consumption. Once public goods exist, they are there for all to enjoy. So it is often the most rational strategy for private actors to let others go first and seek to enjoy the good without contributing to its production. This is a dilemma that public goods face. Without some sort of collective-action mechanism, they risk being underproduced. Conversely, without collective action, public bads—such as pollution, noise, street crime, risky bank lending, and so on—would be over-produced. SE focuses attention on efforts to neutralize the negative effects of externalities associated with the reproduction of racial identities that have the potential to exacerbate interracial conflicts in the United States. Economic discrimination and other forms of disparate treatment serve as means to reduce negative externalities perceived by more powerful groups as emanating from the cultural identity reproduction of less powerful groups (Stewart, 1995).

One of the critical issues addressed by SE analysts is how economic competition among racial groups affects the distribution of goods and opportunities among individuals. When traditional economists think about how members characterized as belonging to the same racial group behave, they often have in mind a form of affiliation similar to voluntary membership in an organization. This perspective has led some commentators to suggest that the historical exploitation of Blacks produced short-term collective efforts to overcome oppression, but no persisting solidarity capable of influencing economic activity. In this view, collective efforts erode once barriers facing individuals are removed.

Stewart (1995, 1976) and Darity, Mason, and Stewart (2003) have developed models that demonstrate how individual decisions regarding economic well-being are influenced by considerations related to racial identity. In these models, the economic opportunities available to an individual agent vary depending on the extent to which active group identification influences that agent's economic decisions. Such choices are, of course, constrained by social custom, history, and other factors. Notions of "white privilege" and "property rights" in whiteness convey the reality that persons socially identified as "White" have a type of "economic safety net" or "group insurance" unavailable to "nonwhites" even if they choose to identify with nonwhites as their primary reference group. Conversely, institutional phenotypic discrimination potentially imposes a type of "tax" on the economic opportunities and outcomes of nonwhites even if their economic behavior and other characteristics mirror those of similarly situated Whites. Governmental action establishes the upper and lower bounds of such taxes. Governmental action can, for example, protect the interests of whites by creating quasi-separate jurisdictions that allow the availability of high-value public goods to be restricted. To illustrate, within some large urban school districts, it is not unusual to find well-endowed public schools populated principally by white students while the majority of schools are resource poor.

As noted previously, collective racial identity is partly an "externality" that has a positive value for those who identify with it or derive benefits unconsciously, but is assessed negatively by those who identify with a different racial/cultural identity or find the cultural production process distasteful for some other reasons. The magnitude of the negative effects generally increases with the frequency and duration of contacts with members of other racial/cultural groups and the degree of overlap in identity characteristics between groups. Some elements of another culture's racial/cultural group identity can be experienced through commodities as opposed to direct contact. Thus, well-designed consumption technologies can allow the positive characteristics of other groups' cultural products to be consumed or experienced, without experiencing the negative external effects associated with direct interaction with the products' originators. The clearest example of this phenomenon is the attraction of suburban white youth who reside in largely segregated enclaves to hip hop music.

Another way of describing these dynamics has been suggested by Okonkwo (1973) who argued the presence of Whites in a particular area who discriminate against Blacks inflicts an external diseconomy on a community of "aware" Blacks. The term "aware" can be interpreted to mean those for whom the production of cultural identity has explicit value. From this vantage point, discriminatory behavior by groups in conflict becomes one manifestation of efforts to adjust the social environment to reduce the impact of perceived externalities associated with cultural production by other groups. Okonkwo, in fact, suggests such an interpretation: "The assumption that discrimination is an externality will in general cut both ways, so that Blacks will appear as a public bad."

Individuals with similar cultural production functions have an incentive to engage in collective behavior to reduce the negative externalities associated with other groups' cultural production. Such intergroup competition can lead to tensions even in the absence of competition for, or maldistribution of, economic resources. It is important to recognize, however, that persisting resource maldistributions will inevitably exacerbate intergroup tensions.

Albert Breton (1974) has shown how individuals will commit resources to political efforts to reduce what he describes as "economic coercion." Economic coercion involves the discomfort or reduced sense of economic well-being experienced by an individual when one's expectations of gains resulting from economic policies deviate from the actual flow of goods and services received. Breton argues that when individuals experience a sufficiently high level of discomfort, they will commit time and resources to political activities in an effort to alter the policy that is perceived to be the source of the discomfort. In a similar vein, individuals and groups will commit economic and noneconomic resources to political activities of various sorts to configure their environments so that cultural identity production can occur without undesired external influences.[1]

The effect of another group's cultural production activities on a person's own-group cultural production thus constitutes a type of quasi-economic coercion that engenders responses similar to those described by Breton. Differences in wealth, or more broadly resource endowments, as well as different traditions of political behavior lead to differences in the types of political activities undertaken by different groups. African Americans often exhibit a preference for political activities like demonstrations because these are relatively lower cost options than paying political lobbyists and allow the intensity of concern to be expressed. In addition, numerical minority status reduces the effectiveness of bloc voting. In contrast, voting is an effective political instrument for whites both because of their numerical majority status (until the mid-twenty-first century) and because the objectives of racial domination and subordination guarantee alignment between actions of elected officials and their individual and collective well-being.

Competition for economic resources is typically layered on top of competition for social space. Thus, when so-called "middle class" Blacks seek to escape the cultural production environment in central cities, they often wind up residing in racially segregated suburban conclaves. In the initial stages of suburban residential demographic transformation, the cultural production of the first Black residents is likely to have little effect on White residents. The income levels and socialization of the initial cohort of Black residents are often more like those of their White counterparts than the Blacks who subsequently relocate to the neighborhood. As cultural production competition intensifies, some Whites will choose to relocate and more will exercise this option as the demographic transition proceeds.

The preceding discussion suggests why school desegregation efforts typically entailed relocation of Black students in relatively small numbers to predominantly white districts. This pattern minimized the negative externalities associated with the activities of the relocated students on white students, while allowing the existing cultural production process to proceed with minimal disruptions. Of course, this policy disrupted the cultural production processes of the relocated Black students.

In general, concentrations of individuals with similar cultural production functions create opportunities to take advantage of economies of scale. As an example, if there are enough residents in a given area a Black church can be established or an independent Black school. Thus the size of the local Black population and its characteristics become important parameters in the location decisions of highly mobile Black professionals. This phenomenon helps explain the high level of Black return migration to the south, and especially magnetic attraction of the Atlanta metropolitan area. In addition, Black middle-class parents are increasingly selecting historically Black institutions of higher education for their offspring although their class status would presumably allow so-called "integrated" options. The goal seems to be to ensure that some minimal level of group identity is produced concurrently with the acquisition of general human capital. Further, parents seek to avoid their children's exposure to the negative externalities and derivative intergroup conflicts associated with cultural production processes operative in many traditionally white institutions.

Cultural production externalities are obviously more important in some activities than in others. These externalities are particularly important in the marriage market, although inter-racial relationships and marriages are increasing. They are also important in competition for positions with high levels of prestige and power, and in the case of religious observances. There is an old adage that the most segregated hour in the week is eleven o'clock on Sunday. Cultural production externalities appear to be least problematic in professional athletics although racial stratification appears to be present in playing positions in some sports and even more so in the ownership, management, and coaching ranks.

The importance of cultural production externalities in the workplace depends on the degree of workers' identification with the profession, organization, and occupation relative to the intensity of their racial group identification. As in athletics, high potential returns from cooperative behavior may overwhelm the effects of negative cultural production externalities. In general, employers attempt to create a quasi-artificial enterprise identity that serves as an alternative or complement to the principal reference groups with which workers identify such as race or religious affiliation. Similar to the process described previously for individuals, this identity is a joint product, that is, an externality generated along with the firm's income-generating activities. Within a bureaucratic organization, individuals are expected to monitor their cultural production so as to minimize the generation of negative externalities that adversely affect productivity and worker solidarity. These expectations create a disproportionate hardship on individuals whose cultural production functions are more dissimilar from the cultural norms. This problem can cut both ways; as an example, a white employee in a Black-owned firm with a majority Black workforce may have to adapt his or her typical cultural production in uncomfortable ways. However, the converse is more typical, that is, Black employees feel pressure to modify cultural identity production to reduce variation from white norms.

The work environment can be structured to minimize the effects of cultural production conflicts on income-generating activities. Various techniques are often used to accomplish this end. As noted previously, racial segregation and occupational crowding were popular strategies during the pre–civil rights movement era. More recently, diversity training has become the principal technique for avoiding intergroup conflicts. Individuals who are unable to modify cultural production functions run the risk of termination and Blacks may well face the most difficult problems in making acceptable adaptations.

Outside the world of work, friendship across racial/cultural groups is feasible to the extent that overt differences in racial identity production are small compared to the collective positive externalities resulting from other sources of affinity. At the same time, it is possible that racial cultural identity production strategies may be bifurcated. Individuals may employ one strategy when dealing face to face with members of another group, while simultaneously making investments in their identity of origin when interacting with family members and other friends. One strategy to avoid cognitive dissonance when employing a bifurcated production strategy is to discount cultural production by someone with a different racial background. One example is the "you are not like those others" syndrome. To some extent, interracial marriages constitute an extreme case of this adaptation strategy. It is important to recognize, however, that distinctive phenotypic characteristics and unique cultural attributes are likely to be always with us. However, the transformation of these attributes into economic property and competing racial identities is not a law of nature, but a close examination of some contemporary patterns of racial inequality suggests that the underlying processes will be difficult to transform.

As noted previously, a second major area of concern is how institutions are organized and operated to achieve acceptable levels of efficiency while simultaneously accommodating patterns of racial domination in institutions that are critical to the normal functioning of the US political economy. In the United States this accommodation involves, among other adaptations, minimizing the degree to which Whites are exposed to undesirable identity production externalities produced by other groups, especially Blacks. Racial disparities and racial discrimination are, then, endemic features of the US economy and social systems. Discrimination based on race, per se, is infused into a myriad of institutional practices in ways that are virtually impossible to totally neutralize or eradicate.

The term "racial stratification" describes the general process by which race is used as a criterion to assign roles and positions in organizations and institutions. Racial stratification in economic institutions leads to the disproportionate assignment of high status positions (those associated with control over allocation of resources, distribution of economic benefits, and high incomes) to members of the dominant group. The collective outcome of the operation of stratification processes across organizations is the institutionalization of a hierarchy of dominant and subordinate statuses among racial groups.

The extent of racial stratification that exists within a given organization or in the society more generally depends, to a major extent, on the balance of political power between dominant and subordinate groups, which may differ across organizations at a given point in time. Structural changes in the economic system, political upheavals, and other major transformative events or processes can disrupt racial stratification processes and alter the short-term balance of political power (create a social disequilibrium). Recognition of the dynamic character of racial stratification processes differentiates the conclusions generated via SE from most other analytical approaches that explore the role of structural forces in perpetuating racial economic inequality. For example, some analysts, including many economists, point to the civil rights movement, subsequent Black electoral gains, and new residential and occupational mobility to declare the formal end of the legacy of historical forms of racial domination/subordination. They claim that discrimination, as typically conceived, is no longer a major factor contributing to the observed racial disparities. Instead, they place the blame for the persistence of these disparities on the victims themselves, i.e., individuals are failing to respond appropriately to market opportunities. The institutions that socialize individuals, e.g., family and friendship networks, are also criticized for encouraging and reinforcing behavior that is unresponsive to market signals and incentives.

From the vantage point of SE, the interventions forced by the civil rights movement were never intended to eliminate previous disparities. Rather, new formal and informal rules, policies, and procedures were instituted in response to changes in the balance of power precipitated by the civil rights movement. While opportunities were created during the early years that indeed did produce some measurable gains, the subsequent reconsolidation of the preexisting racial order reinvigorated racial stratification processes.

The efforts since the mid-1960s to reestablish the previous racial order have involved an intense and ongoing political and legal battle between proponents of equalizing opportunities and adherents to the old racial order. Opponents of equity efforts have masked their objectives in language touting so-called color blind policies. Relentless attacks on so-called Affirmative Action educational and employment policies have mobilized employee resistance to efforts to reduce stratification within organizations and a weakened commitment on the part of managers to reducing stratification.

The willingness of white workers to buy into the anti-stratification reduction rhetoric is driven to a large extent by the need to find a scapegoat for the declining quality of life engendered by globalization pressures. As an example, employers have responded to global competition by reducing benefits for low-income workers. Less than one-fifth of low-income workers have access to employer-sponsored pension plans.

The disruption of the traditional status hierarchy of positions and the angry white male syndrome are particularly prominent since the collapse of Jim Crow in the South. However, backlash against the erosion of white privilege in labor markets has had only limited success, but has crystallized most recently in the emergence of Donald Trump as a disruptive force within the Republican Party touting a thinly veiled call for the restoration of traditional white privilege.

In contrast to the more limited capacity to avoid racial diversity in the workplace, Whites are much more able to avoid interaction with Blacks in residential settings. The efforts of individual Whites to avoid the negative externalities perceived to be associated with Black cultural production are manifested in persistent high levels of racial residential segregation. Hyper-segregation persists despite equal housing legislation and public programs designed to reduce residential segregation. Blacks living in metropolitan areas with Black populations of 1 million or greater are especially likely to live in segregated neighborhoods (Census Scope, n.d.). This pattern simply suggests that higher levels of Black identity production increase incentives for Whites to relocate to avoid negative effects on their own identity production.

Residential segregation contributes to the problem of spatial mismatch. "Spatial mismatch," a term first introduced by economist John Kain in 1968, describes the phenomenon where the suburbanization of jobs coupled with restrictions on the residential options open to blacks created a surplus of workers relative to the available jobs in inner-city neighborhoods resulting in joblessness, lower wages, and longer commutes for black workers. Raphael and Stoll (2002) observe that metropolitan areas with higher levels of black-white residential segregation exhibit a higher degree of spatial mismatch between blacks and jobs. Krovi and Barnes (2000) find that African Americans generally have the longest travel times to work in all regions of the country where public transit is available and that low-income minorities have longer travel times than low-income whites.

It is important to recognize that spatial mismatch patterns are more complex than the historical pattern of inner-city residents having difficulty traveling to suburban job sites. Downward pressure on incomes and status of all workers induced by global competition has trickled down in ways that are intensifying conflicts over valuable commercial and residential space in urban areas. Intense political battles have been and are being waged for control of city government by globalization-friendly constituents who want to make cities more attractive to global corporations.

Compounding the problem of spatial mismatch is the growing presence of new sources of more easily controllable sources of labor to fill low paying, low-status jobs especially in the services sector. The representation of foreign-born workers in the labor force has been growing faster than their population representation, and immigrants are disproportionately employed in business services, construction, nondurable and durable manufacturing, health care, and personal services. SE provides a common sense explanation why immigrants are preferred over domestic Black workers. Immigrants present much less potential status competition than Blacks. The cultural identity production of immigrants is perceived to generate fewer negative externalities for Whites than that of Blacks. Finally, it is easier to maintain social control (racial stratification) through immigration laws and manipulation of residency status.

SE also suggests new ways of understanding mass incarceration of Blacks. It is well known that Black males (and females) are drastically overrepresented in all state prison populations compared to both whites and Hispanics. Many traditional analysts attribute this pattern to disproportionate criminal tendencies among Blacks deriving from the failure of the socializing institutions to cultivate a respect for law and order. However, insights from SE lead to the conclusion that this pattern is itself part and parcel of the system of social control. Cohen and Canelo-Cacho (1994) estimate that the reduction in violent crime due to increases in imprisonment of violent offenders since 1975 has been no more than 10 percent. Spelman (1994) finds that current incarceration rates avert perhaps no more than 8 percent of crimes. One alternative explanation for high Black male incarceration rates is the transformation of this population into economic commodities that are fueling the growth of the prison industrial complex. Many of the new prisons warehousing Blacks are located in rural, predominantly white areas that have lost much of their mining and manufacturing employment bases to industrial shifts. Prisons provide new sources of revenue and the presence of large numbers of Black inmates is acceptable to local white residents because Black cultural production is stringently controlled and status differences between inmates and the local population are sharply defined. In fact, the presence of large populations of Black inmates constitutes a positive input into White cultural identity production as other sources of status have been diminished. More generally, the images of Black criminality in the media, including the infamous "Willie Horton" presidential campaign ad in 1988, fuel White perceptions about the extent of negative externalities associated with Black cultural identity production and reinforce segregation and stratification processes.

Some of the more revealing data suggesting the underlying racial stratification motives associated with incarceration policies are embedded in comparisons of prison operating expenditures per inmate with the costs of educating disadvantaged students. Between 1985 and 1996 state educational expenditure increased by 3.6 percent per year, compared to 7.3 percent for prisons, excluding costs of prison construction (US Bureau of the Census, n.d.). The apparent choice of incarceration over education, even given unfavorable cost-benefit ratios suggests that separating Black males from the population at large serves an important social control function.

While most traditional analysts focus on the analysis of criminal behavior and crime reduction strategies, SE forces us to examine how these patterns interface with various public policies in ways that disrupt Black cultural identity production. Shihadeh and Ousey (1996, 649) maintain that inner-city crime is linked directly to the process of suburbanization, which "contributes to the disinvestments and decline of black communities in the city," increases social isolation, and "thereby engender[s] high crime rates." Clear (1996) argues that incarceration involves the entry and exit of adults from families, leading to a change in economic circumstances of those families, a change that may force relocation. Clear (1996, 9) insists further, "each prisoner represents an economic asset that has been removed from that community and placed elsewhere" who is no longer spending money in the community. Moreover, most ex-offenders are likely to return to their neighborhoods upon release and "these ex-offenders are more likely to be unemployed or underemployed, adding to the local unemployment rate and the chronic difficulties ex-convicts face in finding and retaining work" (Clear 1996, 9).

While the preceding discussion provides only a partial overview of the range of stratification processes with which SE is concerned, it demonstrates that this framework of analysis provides a more comprehensive analysis of the dynamics of racial stratification than its competitors and can thus facilitate in the development of more functional strategies to change the status quo.

CONCLUSION

SE suggests several fundamental issues that must be addressed in efforts to develop strategies to combat racial stratification and intergroup conflict. First, in a world characterized by cultural differences and inequitable distribution of economic resources, intergroup conflict in both economic and noneconomic settings is an endogenous characteristic of the social space rather than an exogenous contaminant of market allocation processes and individual decision-making. Second, collective identity has economic value and groups will forego income and wealth to protect identity production. Third, reductions in intergroup income and wealth differentials will not automatically lead to the erosion of traditional patterns of collective identification. Fourth, as long as investments in racial identity generate differential returns for different identities significant racial stratification will persist. Fifth, incentives for engaging in cooperative intergroup behavior can reduce the potentially negative dimensions of inter-racial contact and create alternatives to traditional racial identification. And sixth, movement toward more egalitarian inter- and intra-racial distributions of wealth must be a major element in any earnest attempt to reduce racial conflict.

By specifying the mechanisms through which racial inequalities are perpetuated the subfield of SE provides a valuable blueprint for additional research. Further analyses employing stratification paradigms have the potential to produce new insights regarding strategies to achieve significant reductions in inter-racial economic inequality.

NOTE

1. Cultural identity or identity production is the process by which cultural identity is created. The cultural production function might include inputs such as modes of speech or dress, choices of entertainment and food, and neighborhood location.

BIBLIOGRAPHY

Arrow, Kenneth. 1974. "The Theory of Discrimination." In *Discrimination in Labor Markets*, edited by Orley Ashenfelter & Albert Rees. Princeton, NJ: Princeton University Press.

Becker, Gary. 1957. *The Economics of Discrimination*. Chicago: University of Chicago Press.

Breton, Albert. 1974. *The Economic Theory of Representative Government*. Chicago: Aldine Publishing Company.

Census Scope. n.d. *Segregation Dissimilarity Indices, US Metro Areas Ranked by White/Black Dissimilarity Index*. http://www.censusscope.org/us/rank_dissimilarity_white_black.html.

Clear, Todd. 1996. Backfire: When Incarceration Increases Crime. http://www.doc.state.ok.us/DOCS/OCJRC/Ocjrc96/Ocjrc7.htm.

Cohen, Jacqueline and Jose Canela-Cacho. 1994. "Incapacitation and Violent Crime." In *Understanding and Preventing Violence,* edited by Albert Reiss and Jeffrey Roth, 296–338. Washington, DC: National Academy of Sciences.

Coleman, Major G. 2003. "African American Popular Wisdom Versus the Qualification Question: Is Affirmative Action Merit-based." *Western Journal of Black Studies* 27: 35–44.

Darity, William, Patrick Mason and James Stewart. 2003. The Economics of Identity: The Origin and Persistence of Racial Norms. (Mimeo).

Darity, William and Rhonda Williams. 1985. "Peddlers Forever?: Culture, Competition, and Discrimination," *Papers and Proceedings of the American Economic Review* 75(2): 256–261.

Du Bois, William E. B. 1903. *The Souls of Black Folk, Essays and Sketches*. Chicago: A. C. McClurg & Co.

Inadequate Funding Makes NCLB Worse. 2003. *FairTest Examiner*. (Winter-Spring). Accessed at http://fairtest.org/examarts/Wint-Spring%2003%20double/Funding.html.

Kain, John. 1968. "Housing Segregation, Negro Employment, and Metropolitan Decentralization," *Quarterly Journal of Economics* 82: 175–197.

Krovi, Ravindra and Claude Barnes. 2000. Work-related Travel Patterns of People of Color. In *Travel Patterns of People of Color*. Columbus, OH: Battelle.

Mason, Patrick L. 1995. "Race, Competition, and Differential Wages," *Cambridge Journal of Economics* 19(4): 545–568.

———. 1997. "Race, Culture, and Skill: Interracial Wage Differences Among African Americans, Latinos, and Whites." *The Review of Black Political Economy* 25: 5–39.

———. 1999. "Competing Explanations of Male Interracial Wage Differentials: Missing Variables Models Versus Job Competition." *Cambridge Journal of Economics* (May).

———. 2003. "Persistent Racial Discrimination in the Labor Market," this volume.

Okonkwo, Ubadigbo. 1973. "The Economics of Ethnic Discrimination," *The Review of Black Political Economy* 3(2): 1–18.

Raphael, Steven and Michael Stoll. 2002. *Modest Progress: The Narrowing Spatial Mismatch Between Blacks and Jobs in the 1990s.* The Living Census Series. Washington, DC: The Brookings Institution.

Shihadeh, Edward and Graham Ousey. 1996. "Metropolitan expansion and Black Social Dislocation: The Link Between Suburbanization and Center-City Crime." *Social Forces* 75(2): 649–666.

Spelman, William. 1994. *Criminal Incapacitation.* New York: Plenum.

Stephan, James. 1999. *State Prison Expenditures, 1996.* Washington, DC: U.S. Department of Justice. NCJ 172211 (August).

Stewart, James. 1976. *An Analysis of the Impacts of Structural Variables on the Relative Levels of Economic Welfare of the Black Populations of the United States and the Republic of South Africa.* Ph.D. Dissertation, Department of Economics, University of Notre Dame.

———. 1995. "Toward Broader Involvement of Black Economists in Discussions of Race and Public Policy: A Plea for a Reconceptualization of Race and Power in Economic Theory, NEA Presidential Address, 1994," *The Review of Black Political Economy* 23(3): 13–36.

U.S. Bureau of the Census. n.d. *State Government Finances, 1985—96.* http://www.ojp.usdoj.gov/bjs/pub/pdf/spe96.pdf.

U.S. Bureau of the Census. 2001. Profile of the Foreign-Born Population in the United States: 2000. *Current Population Reports.* Special Studies. Report P23–206. Washington, DC: U.S. Government Printing Office.

Williams, R. 1991. "Competition, Discrimination and Differential Wage Rates: On the Continued Relevance of Marxian Theory to the Analysis of Earnings and Employment Inequality." In *New Approaches to the Economic and Social Analysis of Discrimination,* edited by R. Cornwall and P. Wunnava, 65–92. New York: Praeger.

Chapter 7

A New Era for Labor?

The Promises and Perils of the Fast Food Workers Strike Movement

Marcia Walker-McWilliams

It began on November 29, 2012, in New York City when about 200 workers from some thirty fast food restaurants staged a strike against their employers. In the weeks, months, and years to follow, thousands of workers across 190 US cities have staged workplace demonstrations, strikes, marches, and peaceful protests in and outside of fast food restaurants. Their demands were many, but the most consistent demands included the right to collectively bargain and unionize, a $15 hourly wage, and overall better working conditions, benefits, and respect. Soon, gas station attendants, grocery store workers, home health aides, personal care attendants, and workers in big box stores like Walmart joined the fight for a livable wage and greater worker's rights. To some, it was the dawn of a brand new era for America's down-but-not-out labor movement. Others argued that unskilled workers in the low-wage service sector had no right to demand a higher wage in a struggling economy where college graduates faced uncertain job prospects.

As a scholar of African American and labor history, I was fascinated by the surge in worker activism and could not help but notice the stark ways in which race, class, and gender were at the crux of not only the debate as to whether or not these workers had a justifiable cause, but how frequently people of color, especially black women and men, were on the front lines of these demonstrations. Their signs read "Fairer Wages. Safer Workplaces. Dignity and Respect for All" as well as "On Strike: Can't Survive on $7.25." In New York, the signs of black workers read, "I am a Man" and "I am a Woman," clearly referencing the 1968 Memphis sanitation workers strike in which black men called for dignity, fair working conditions, and the right to unionize. At other strikes, black women held pictures of Rosa Parks, and in Atlanta veteran civil rights activist and US Congressman John Lewis posed with five young black women at a rally. The women's signs read "Stop corporate greed" and "Fight for \$15." To further highlight the connections between black men and women on the front lines of the fast food workers movement and civil rights, several demonstrators held signs that read "Black Lives Matter." In short, seeking a livable wage, fair working conditions, and the right to collectively bargain with employers was not solely about economics but about civil rights.

Should black Americans care about these workers and this movement? Yes. Black Americans are both producers and consumers in the fast food industry and the service economy. Black workers represent about 17 percent of the fast food workforce and about 28 percent of all black women work in the service sector (US Bureau of Labor Statistics 2012). As consumers in a growing service economy, black Americans should care not only about the cost of goods but also the costs of growing income inequality. The high density of fast food establishments in black communities and the politics of consumption mandate that blacks consider whether and how funds spent in their communities' cycle back to them in measurable ways, including livable wages for those who constitute the working poor. While gains in education, equal employment opportunities and entrepreneurship have opened up pathways for greater mobility, these avenues are not as clear and accessible for blacks who occupy low-wage jobs in the growing service economy where there is limited opportunity for advancement. Thus, we must consider and take seriously the fast food workers movement and the place of black Americans within it as well as their place in US labor history and the service economy.

THE LONG HISTORY OF BLACK WORKER ACTIVISM

The recognition of one's right to his or her own labor, the ability to make an adequate living, and the right to live an economically autonomous life have been central pursuits in African American freedom struggles since enslavement. In the years after emancipation, black men and women utilized organizations like the Freedmen's Bureau to establish voluntary contracts with employers, although with decidedly mixed results as the terms of these contracts were typically in favor of white employers. Barred from many industries, blacks were able to join a relatively small number of craft-based unions and often only in segregated locals (Jacobson 1968). The most prominent labor union of the era, the National Labor Union, reflecting societal prejudices, refused to take an integrationist stance and truly represent black workers. Determined to establish inclusive labor organizations that would represent them, blacks formed their own trade unions and even established the Colored National Labor Union in 1869. Black workers constantly compared their challenges with procuring equal employment opportunities and decent wages as free men and women to their experiences under enslavement. How different was freedom from enslavement when blacks lacked true economic determination?

Although most craft and trade unions were predominantly male, black women also organized for fair wages, safe working conditions, dignity, and respect. Scholar Tera Hunter's *To 'Joy My Freedom: Southern Black Women's Lives and Labors after the Civil War* (1998) explored in depth black women's efforts to establish baselines for their wages and treatment as domestic workers and laundresses, evidenced by their demands to live outside of the homes of their employees and in their own communities. Hunter argues, "Women's success or frustrations in influencing the character of domestic labor would define how meaningful freedom would be ... a free labor system required rethinking assumptions about work that had previously relied on physical coercion" (Hunter 1998, 26). When black women were not paid, mistreated on the job, held to long hours, or subject to sexual and physical abuse, they exercised the option to quit and seek employment elsewhere: "Occasional refusals to sell their labor or self-imposed limits enabled working-class women to conduct their own family and community affairs in ways that mitigated the demands of white supremacy and the market economy" (Hunter 1998, 28). Navigating freedom meant navigating a complex set of race- and gender-based restrictions.

The early twentieth century opened up greater employment opportunities for working-class blacks, though most were concentrated in the agrarian sector as sharecroppers and tenant farmers, were domestic workers (heavily African American female), held service positions, or were unemployed. (General studies that focus exclusively or predominantly on the first half of the twentieth century include Harris 1982; Jacobson 1968; Honey 2000; Cayton and Mitchell 1939; Foner 1989.) The first wave of the Great Migration, from about 1910 to 1930, spurred black movement into urban and northern industrial centers, a pattern that increased during World War I as employers sought native white and black workers to replace a reduced immigrant workforce. At the time, the most dominant labor organization was the American Federation of Labor (AFL), founded by Samuel Gompers in 1881. The AFL maintained an official policy of nondiscrimination toward black workers, but in reality it failed to sanction the lily-white policies of its affiliate unions that barred blacks from representation and actively fought against the hiring of black workers, not only as strikebreakers but also as permanent workers. For those blacks who were unionized in the AFL, they were more than likely in segregated locals. The failure of the AFL to rebuke racism in its locals and discrimination in hiring, promotion, and representation prompted black workers to question the benefits of organized labor even more than they previously had.

Preeminent black labor leader A. Philip Randolph organized black porters and maids employed with the Pullman Company into the Brotherhood of Sleeping Car Porters in 1925. About ten years later, the Brotherhood of Sleeping Car Porters officially became an affiliate of the AFL and Randolph soon gained a position on its executive board which was under the leadership of George Meany. Randolph became the voice of antidiscrimination in the AFL, a position that Meany resented. Randolph was a labor man, loyal to the principles of trade unionism, but he also believed that in order for organized labor to be at its strongest, it could not afford to discriminate against workers of color who were becoming more and more of a factor in industrial employment. Furthermore, by 1936, black workers had an alternative to the AFL with the formation of the Congress of Industrial Organizations (CIO), which catered more toward workers in industrial workspaces as opposed to the predominantly (white) craft unionism of the AFL. The CIO pledged antidiscrimination in its charter and policies but took it a step further by actually endorsing and organizing interracial locals within unions like the United Packinghouse Workers of America (UPWA) and the United Auto Workers (UAW). Whereas the interracial organizing attempts of the nineteenth-century Knights of Labor were less successful, the formation of the CIO and its interracial organizing helped usher in a period of an increasing black presence in the organized labor movement.

American involvement in World War II brought increased employment opportunities for women and minorities, particularly in the industrial workforce. Women and minorities filled many of the positions left open by men who enlisted in the war, but they also filled new positions created by the demand for wartime goods and artillery. Despite their increased numbers, the racial and gender barriers of industrial employment and organized labor remained difficult to penetrate. Black workers often faced "hate strikes" in which white workers would walk off the job and refuse to work if a black person integrated their departments. In industries like meatpacking, positions were typically classified by gender ("men's work" vs. "women's work") but also by race (jobs for black men and black women as opposed to jobs for white men and white women). Typically, the jobs for black men and women were dirtier, more dangerous, and paid less than those of their white counterparts. Randolph was particularly militant and vocal about the discriminatory practices evident not only within the hiring and classification of workers in general but in the organizing of unions at the local and national levels. Randolph melded his concern for economic and civil rights in the organized labor movement with his desire to see change take shape on a national level. Black workers and civil rights pushed for the Double V campaign—victory or democracy abroad and at home—to call attention to the hypocrisy of fighting Hitler and fascism abroad while doing nothing about racism at home. Randolph spearheaded the March on Washington Movement in 1941 which pushed President Franklin D. Roosevelt to pass the Fair Employment Act and create the Fair Employment Practices Commission (FEPC), which had moderate success in curbing racial discrimination in the hiring and employment of workers in defense industries. (For more on A. Philip Randolph's life and the relationship between blacks, civil rights, and organized labor in the 1940s and 1950s, see Anderson 1972; Pfeffer 1990; Foner 1981; Kersten 2000; Korstad 2003; Liechtenstein 1982; Lipsitz 1994; Zieger 1995; Bynum 2010.)

But in the postwar reconversion process, blacks fell victim to the practice of "last hired, first fired" and were laid off at higher rates than their white counterparts. For those who were able to maintain their jobs, promotions were extremely difficult to obtain as too often blacks were frozen out of promotion channels. American unions came under attack as communist fronts in the postwar era of red-baiting and suffered some key blows. Chief among these blows was the passage of the 1947 Taft-Hartley Act, which restricted the rights of unions and organized workers. Though there were some communists in organized labor, workers who defended and fought for integrated locals and antidiscrimination faced allegations of communism. Many black workers melded their concern for fair and equal employment in the workplace with concerns for civil rights and equality in society. A number of black labor activists, including A. Philip Randolph, Addie Wyatt, Charles Hayes, and Maida Springer Kemp, understood that the paths of organized labor and civil rights activism were connected for black workers. In fact, the work of black labor activists in forming integrated local unions and workspaces in the 1930s, 1940s, and 1950s, as well as equal consideration in hiring, promotions, and pay, provided valuable insight and strategies for local and national civil rights struggles. The perspectives of black labor activists often differed significantly from mainstream labor leadership.

The topmost level of the organized labor–civil rights relationship may be analyzed through the AFL-CIO's official position on civil rights. George Meany became president of the AFL-CIO in 1955 when the AFL and CIO merged. The AFL was conservative in its race politics, and many of its unions restricted African Americans from membership. Founded to challenge the AFL, the CIO was more racially progressive and radically oriented. The National Association for the Advancement of Colored People (NAACP) supported the merger of the AFL-CIO in 1955 and Meany and the AFL-CIO leadership on the surface supported civil rights measures and legislation, but the practices and policies of a number of its unions actively promoted or overlooked discrimination against workers of color. Some AFL-CIO unions did provide financial support to civil rights organizations but did so on an uneven basis. (In *The New Left and Labor in the 1960s* [1994], Peter Levy argues that AFL-CIO's Committee on Political Education [COPE] sent funds to the Student Nonviolent Coordinating Committee [SNCC] and that progressive unions the UPWA and UAW raised funds for SNCC from 1961 through 1963. However, the delegitimized, more radical elements of the civil rights movement received little funds from labor and white liberal supporters. In "Organized Labor and the Civil Rights Movement of the 1960s: The Case of the Maryland Freedom Union" [1990], Michael Flug argues that civil rights organizations like the NAACP, SCLC, SNCC, and CORE made demands on organized labor that ranged from "financial, legislative, and political support" as well as demands to enforce antidiscriminatory hiring and employment practices and to organize unorganized workers.)

Thus the relationship between organized labor and civil rights at the topmost level rested on an uneven balance. Black workers within the AFL-CIO still faced discrimination, whereas some civil rights organizations like the Council on Racial Equality (CORE) were grounded in black working-class grassroots supports and other organizations, particularly the NAACP, have been critiqued for pursuing a middle-class integrationist agenda while downplaying black working-class issues such as blue-collar antidiscrimination activism. (Risa Golubuff argues that in the 1940s, black working-class support of the NAACP grew and the NAACP actively pursued antidiscrimination labor legislation and that legal notions of civil rights were infused with the concerns of workers. Yet when the NAACP switched its civil rights tactics from fighting for specific labor legislation to rejecting labor cases and pushing for school desegregation, the needs of black working-class workers were overlooked. See Goluboff 2005.)

The uneasy alliance between labor and civil rights organizations such as the NAACP, CORE, SNCC, and SCLC was dynamic to say the least. The alliance would be strengthened and weakened throughout the course of the civil rights movement. A particularly tense moment came with the publishing of NAACP labor secretary Herbert Hill's "Racism within Organized Labor: A Report of Five Years of the AFL-CIO" in 1960. Hill offered a scathing critique of the AFL-CIO for adopting antidiscrimination clauses in its constitution but making little effort to actually enforce the antidiscrimination policies in its affiliates. Hill argued that discrimination in the AFL-CIO took four forms: "outright exclusion of blacks, segregated locals, separate racial seniority lines in collective bargaining agreements and exclusion of blacks from apprenticeship training programs controlled by labor unions" (Hill 1961). Racially segregated affiliates and local chapters of unions operated all over the south and in many northern industries as well. Though Hill was and still remains a controversial figure, "Racism in organized labor" signaled to black workers and the labor movement that labor concerns, if never the focal point of the NAACP's legislative agenda remained within the purview of its leadership as a prime concern for black constituents (MacLean 2004; see also Hill 1961).

In 1960, Randolph, upset with the lack of progress toward antidiscrimination within the AFL-CIO, founded the Negro American Labor Council to act as a base within organized labor for black activists to air their grievances, organize black workers, and support black labor leadership. At the local level, the Chicago chapter of the National Association of Letter Carriers (NALC) was particularly militant in its pursuit for greater black membership and leadership. The Chicago chapter of the NALC also devoted significant funds and organizing support to the civil rights struggles in Chicago as well as in the south. The Chicago chapter of the NALC as well as labor unions like the UPWA in Chicago were some of the first to recognize and provide financial and legal support to Martin Luther King Jr.'s Montgomery bus boycott (Proceedings of the Montgomery, Alabama Bus Boycott Conference 1956). In addition black workers and their labor allies lent human and financial capital to the family of Emmitt Till after his murder, to blacks displaced from their homes for registering to vote in Fayette County, Tennessee, and to those participating in the Selma-to-Montgomery voting rights marches. In Chicago, black labor activists protested racist school policies, police brutality, and segregated retailers and restaurants and stumped for racially progressive political candidates. Despite the sometimes tense relationship between the top levels of organized labor leadership and racist unions and workers, black workers and their allies were key constituents and supporters of civil rights. James Farmer, director of CORE, argued at the UPWA's 1963 Legislation and Civil Rights Conference that the civil rights movement had borrowed its protest tactics of marches, sit-ins, and organizing from the labor movement. Farmer also asserted that "the very same people who are anti-civil rights are the folk who are pushing for the so-called right-to-work laws. The natural alliance [between labor and the civil rights movement] should not be broken" (Levy 1994, 9; see also "Transcript of Civil Rights and Legislative Conference" 1963). Furthermore, the 1963 March on Washington, inspired by Randolph's 1941 movement, was in fact the March on Washington for *Jobs* and Freedom.

The centrality of fair and adequate work opportunities to the civil rights movement must be underscored, and we cannot overlook the centrality of civil rights to black workers and organized labor. The 1964 Civil Rights Act, which barred discrimination in the workplace on the basis of race and sex, and the formation of the Equal Employment Opportunity Commission (EEOC), which investigated claims of workplace discrimination, created a legal space for black men and women to contest unfair treatment. Many of the first cases brought before the EEOC were on behalf of black women who argued that they had been discriminated against based on their race and sex.

Black women and men challenged their exclusion from retail, service, and professional lines of work not only on the basis of their strong consumerism but supported by equal employment legislation and continued civil rights activism.

By the 1970s, African Americans had higher rates of unionization than whites, but struggled to obtain leadership positions within their unions and at the top levels of the AFL-CIO. The situation was even more dire for black women in organized labor who faced barriers on the basis of their race and sex. In certain industries, such as building construction, blacks faced extreme exclusion from trade education programs, hiring pipelines, and union representation. Groups like the Coalition of Black Trade Unionists, founded in 1972, understood the plight of black organized and unorganized workers and bridged labor, civil rights, and political action. Coalition of Black Trade Unionists (CBTU) made its attempts to bridge the plight of black workers in the labor movement to broader concerns about the economic and political struggles of black and poor families. CBTU sought to "work cooperatively and actively with church, social, civic, education and civil rights organizations to improve the living conditions of black and poor families, and that black trade unionists seek out opportunities to serve on local boards and commissions in order to maximize the participation and influence of black and poor workers in community decision-making" (CBTU Convention Proceedings 1972).

The 1970s and 1980s were a pivotal time for organized labor. At the same time, organized labor became more bureaucratic, with labor leadership further removed from its grassroots base, which demographically reflected a growing female and minority workforce. Higher-wage jobs in manufacturing and production declined in the United States and what was left of the industry steadily moved further south to southern states that were by and large less hospitable to unions. The anti-union policies of the Reagan administration also contributed to the decline of American labor during this period. As manufacturing declined, the United States increasingly moved toward a service-oriented consumer economy. Still, the growth of black workers in retail, grocery, and service positions constituted a key constituency that needed to be organized. Many of these workers, younger and located in the South, were in areas where attempts to unionize were openly discouraged and could result in intimidation and the loss of one's job. In addition, many faced right-to-work laws in their states that limited the power of unions to represent workers. The decline in power and membership of the American labor movement and the shift toward a more service-oriented economy had dramatic effects on the ways in which black workers could organize for greater economic and political power, particularly because chronic and cyclical unemployment often placed them outside of the workforce entirely.

(The literature on the decline of American labor movement and its effects on urban centers on working-class people has grown in recent years. See Sugrue 1996; Wilson 1987, 1997, Thompson 2001; Nelson 2001; Moody 1988; Bluestone and Harrison 1982.)

But labor and black working-class protests were not dead. The decade of the 1990s witnessed continued pressure on behalf of black and minority workers for increased wages, the opportunity to unionize, and better working conditions and benefits. Perhaps nowhere was this most evident than in the 1990 Delta Pride Catfish strike in Mississippi. In the Mississippi Delta, about 40 percent of all blacks fall below the federal poverty line. Many of the jobs available to them existed in the low-wage service sector and food-processing industries, most notably in the multimillion-dollar catfishing industry where the average catfish worker received a little less than $4 per hour. At Delta Pride, one of the largest catfish processing plants in the nation, a workforce of predominantly working-class black women struggled for dignity, respect, fair wages, benefits, and working conditions. The grievances of the women in particular revolved around sexual harassment in the plant and an archaic, inhumane bathroom policy in which male supervisors followed women into the bathrooms, which had had the doors removed from their stalls. Women resorted to forming "human doors" in order to give some semblance of privacy (Zook 2006, 161–163; White and Hollins 1995).

In addition, women complained of male bosses and supervisors who would touch them inappropriately or verbally abuse them. Leave and sick time were virtually nonexistent and medical treatment for the high incidences of carpal tunnel syndrome due to the fast-paced, monotonous motion of beheading and preparing catfish, consisted of a nurse who would give out Tylenol or pain medication. Workers routinely stood for hours in ankle-deep water filled with blood and fish entrails and many complained of eye, throat, and skin irritation due to the high levels of ammonia in the plant's water system. Complaints went unheard, and those who spoke out against the working conditions were terminated or demoted. Given that management and ownership of Delta Pride was predominantly white and its underpaid, poorly treated workforce largely black, conditions within the plants were deemed as little more than plantations with walls ("Women's Pride at Delta Pride" 1991).

Determined to bring in a living wage and work under healthy, dignified, and fair conditions, several black women, including Sarah White, Margaret Hollins, Rose Turner, and Mary Young, led a successful organizing campaign and the plant was eventually unionized in 1986 with the formation of United Food and Commercial Workers (UFCW) Local 1529. But a poor contract, lack of progress in pay and working conditions, and a failure to agree upon terms in 1990 led to a strike. The strike soon garnered national attention and sparked boycotts against Delta Pride spearheaded by civil rights organizations like the NAACP, Operation PUSH in Chicago, and other allies within the labor movement and the Mississippi Delta. Despite intimidation and violence toward striking workers, the hiring of strikebreakers, and other company tactics to break the strike, the men and women on strike withstood these efforts. After a three-month strike, the company agreed to negotiate with the union for a new contract. The new contract includes a wage increase over three years, the creation of a joint management/worker safety committee, increased benefits and more vacation time, as well as unlimited bathroom privileges and an improved grievance procedure ("Women's Pride at Delta Pride" 1991). The strike and the efforts of black workers to fight for dignity and respect on the job, with some success, are important to note. While their new wages in catfish processing would not pull black workers out of poverty, the significance of their struggle cannot be overlooked.

A NEW ERA? FAST FOOD, THE NEW SERVICE ECONOMY, AND BLACK WORKERS

The history of black working-class and labor activism in the United States is rich indeed and inextricably linked to civil rights struggles and the pursuit of black freedom and dignity. The black men and women at the forefront of the fast food workers movement should be understood within the context of this historical relationship. At the same time, the circumstances of their positions within the service industry require a nuanced analysis. Fast food and service workers are operating within a US and global economy far different from the postwar economy. Within the past twenty years, numerous scholars and journalists have chronicled the rise of what they term the "low-wage nation." In *Nickel and Dimed: On (Not) Getting By in America* (2001), Barbara Ehrenreich, an educated white woman, went undercover to work five different low-wage jobs: as a waitress, hotel maid, house cleaner, home health aid, and Walmart worker. Her goal was to see how it is that the working poor survive and ultimately found that survival was based on having not one low-wage job but multiple low-wage jobs. She noted the lack of health care and other benefits for workers, the mental and physical difficulties of low-wage employment, high levels of homelessness, as well as the instability of service jobs and high turnover rates. Eric Schlosser's *Fast Food Nation* (2001) and David Shipler's *The Working Poor* (2004) came to similar conclusions about the plight of America's millions of workers in poverty.

In December of 2014, two years after the start of the fast food workers movement, the *Boston Globe* profiled the lives of several fast food workers, one of which was a young single African American mother, Latiana Holmes. Holmes held three jobs, sometimes working over 70 hours per week. Her jobs included regular shifts at a Dunkin Donuts, an overnight security guard position at Northeastern University, and as a personal care attendant (Johnston 2014). In her best months, Holmes could pull in $2,400 a month, or about $30,000 a year. But this came at a cost. She had little to no time to spend with her two-year-old son and lived with her disabled mother and two siblings in order to have child care and a regular residence. She had hoped to work and attend school, but dropped out of college because tuition was too high. With no car, Holmes had to rely on public transportation to get to and from her three jobs. Still, her hold on these jobs was tenuous. She temporarily lost her job at Dunkin Donuts after she missed a shift due to a medical emergency with her son and worried about the long-term effects of being gone all of the time on her relationship with her son.

Holmes's story is just one portrait of those working in the fast food industry, trying to make ends meet in today's growing service economy. Fast food workers on strike argue that low wages have led to evictions, perpetual homelessness, and the need to rely on elderly and indigent family and friends for housing. Workers cite extreme hours and a lack of leave time that prohibit them from seeing their family, raising their children, and playing a more active role in their communities. There are an estimated 4.5 million fast food workers and about 85 percent of them are American born. Though 59 percent are white, blacks are overrepresented in the fast food industry. While blacks make up about 12 percent of the US population, they make up about 17 percent of fast food workers and Latinos represent 19 percent (Schmitt and Jones 2013). Yet even though they are not the majority of fast food workers, black men and women have been at the forefront of organizing and leading the movement though groups like Strike Fast Food, Fast Food Forward (funded by the Service Employees International Union), and Fight for $15 campaigns in numerous cities. In addition, many workers have staged autonomous demonstrations, sometimes in conjunction with groups like Black Lives Matter, and have often merged their concerns of workplace and economic justice to struggles against police brutality and racial injustice writ large, much like previous generations of black labor activists. In New York, St. Louis, Chicago, and other cities across the nation, black fast food workers have included "I Can't Breathe" die-ins and "Hands Up" marches in reference to the police murders of Eric Garner and Michael Brown during strikes and demonstrations against their employers.

Visually, race has been an important as well as understated feature of the fast food workers movement. But what has garnered the most attention is the movement's major demand of a $15 per hour wage. The current federal minimum wage (since 2009) stands at $7.25 which would amount to a little over $15,000 in annual wages working full time. Many workers argue that this keeps them in a perpetual cycle of poverty. The US Bureau of Labor

Statistics calculated that the mean, or average, wage for fast food workers as well as gas station cashiers, grocery, restaurant and recreation workers was about $9.07 an hour, amounting to just under $19,000 a year, assuming a full-time work schedule. This just meets the federal poverty line for a family of three. President Obama's proposal to raise the federal minimum wage to $10.10 an hour has been cited by some as more palatable and feasible than demands for $15 an hour, while others have argued that any increase in the minimum wage will be the death nail for small businesses employing service and low-wage workers. A $15 hourly wage could yield about $31,000 in annual wages for full-time work before taxes. Fast food workers claim that this would be enough to lift the working poor and their families above the federal poverty line.

Extreme fatigue along with health problems and a lack of paid leave, sick leave, or time off have also been cited by workers as issues that the movement seeks to address. According to a 2013 study conducted by the Center for Labor Research and Education at the University of California, Berkeley, only about 13 percent of fast food workers receive benefits of some kind (Allegretto et al. 2013). For workers, the situation amounts to one in which the fast food industry perpetuates growing income inequality and the chasm between the haves and have-nots in America. The National Employment Law Project found that in 2012, the profits of the seven largest publicly traded fast food organizations were astronomical compared with the wages of workers. McDonalds, Pizza Hut, KFC, Subway, Burger King, Wendy's, Dunkin Donuts, and Dairy Queen were among some of the top-earning fast food companies and brought in over $7.44 billion, paid their top executives $52.7 million, and doled out $7.7 billion in dividends, stocks, and buybacks as their workers began to take to the streets for higher wages and the right to unionize (National Employment Law Project 2013).

Despite these findings, fast food workers have faced an uphill battle in terms of battling public perception when it comes to their demands. One criticism of the fast food workers movement derives from the argument that even presumably skilled and highly educated college graduates face uncertain economic prospects in today's economy, so why should less-educated and presumably less-skilled workers receive higher wages. They argue that these workers should have made better decisions by gaining more education, having fewer children, or gaining skills that would allow them to achieve more desirable, higher-paying employment. Others maintain the argument a majority of fast food workers are in fact high school students. But according to a study by the Center for Economic and Policy Research, only about 30 percent of fast food workers are high school age, while the majority are twenty years of age and older. The median age for fast food workers is twenty-eight years old, and of those who are not teenagers, 85 percent have a high school diploma and about a third have taken some college courses (Center for Economic and Policy Research 2013). In short, workers in the fast food industry today are older and better educated than many believe. Furthermore, about 25 percent of fast food workers have children and are raising a family on their wages.

Other critics fear that the demand for a $15 hourly wage would sink small businesses who would not only have to pay workers more but also comply with federal healthcare mandates under the Affordable Care Act. The jury is still out on these claims as the long-term effects of the Affordable Care Act have yet to be seen, and even then disaggregating the cause of small business failure is complicated as many factors have to be taken into account. What also remains to be seen is what effects a higher minimum wage will have on the plight of low-wage workers and local economies. The protests of fast food workers have not gone unnoticed in cities like Seattle, Chicago, and San Francisco where city legislatures have pledged to increase the minimum wages of their municipalities anywhere from $13 to $15 over the next several years. Additional cities are mulling over the prospects of raising their minimum wages, but according to the cost of living, rather than a standardized $15 per hour wage.

Arguments in favor of increasing local minimum wages include a desire to increase the standard of living and purchasing power of those who work in the service industry. But city leaders are also trying to solve pressing financial concerns and hope that by placing more fiscal responsibility onto businesses, the amount of government aid given to the working poor will decrease. According to a study by the Center for Labor Research and Education, low wages and a lack of benefits for fast food workers cost American taxpayers $3.9 billion in Medicaid and CHIP benefits, $1.95 billion in Earned Income Tax Credit (EITC) benefits, about $1 billion in food stamps, and $82 million in Temporary Assistance for Needy Families (TANF). While 25 percent of the American workforce receives some sort of public aid, 52 percent of fast food workers are enrolled in one or more public aid programs (Center for Labor Research and Education 2013). The states that had to subsidize the fast food industry the most include California, New York, Texas, Illinois, and Florida.

CONCLUSION

The fast food workers movement is unfolding daily, and much remains to be seen as to what the successes and challenges of the movement will be in the long run. According to the Alliance for Justice, about 48 percent of job growth in the United States is projected to be in the low-wage service sector in retail, food service, and freight work. About 40 percent of those jobs are projected to pay less than $15 per hour (Alliance for a Just Society 2013). If anything, the fast food workers strike movement raises important questions about American ideals and realities. What happens when full-time work does not lead to a comfortable living and stability but rather poverty? Is it the fault of less-educated, less-skilled workers? Are corporations and companies intent on more and more profits to blame? When the working poor become the undeserving poor, how does it change our understandings of the value of work, the purpose of education, and the economic viability of the United States?

For black Americans, these questions are even more salient. Nearly one out of three black women work in the service sector. The stability of working-class communities and communities of color, where more may be living from one paycheck to the next, has to be considered in order to understand urban and racial poverty. Low-wage work does not have only short-term effects but also long-term effects when one considers the cycle of poverty created by a lack of savings, retirement funds, and the overall inability to build wealth in black communities for future generations. Black members of the fast food workers movement know that the stakes are high and have banded together in an interracial alliance with other workers to challenge the conditions of their labor. They have built upon not only the Occupy Wall Street movement and growing critiques of economic inequality but upon a much longer history of black labor activism that has understood freedom to encompass economic viability in addition to political, civil, and social rights.

BIBLIOGRAPHY

Allegretto, Sylvia A., Marc Doussard, Dave Graham-Squire, Ken Jacobs, Dan Thompson and Jeremy Thompson. 2013. *Fast Food, Poverty Wages: The Public Cost of Low-Wage Jobs in the Fast-Food Industry.* UC Berkeley Center for Labor Research and Education, October 15.
Anderson, Jervis. 1972. *A. Philip Randolph: A Biographical Portrait.* New York: Harcourt Brace Jovanovich.
Bluestone, Barry, and Bennett Harrison. 1982. *The Deindustrialization of America: Plant Closings, Community Abandonment and the Dismantling of Basic Industries.* New York: Basic Books.
Bynum, Cornelius. 2010. *A. Philip Randolph and the Struggle for Civil Rights.* Urbana: University of Illinois Press.
Cayton, Horace, and George Mitchell. 1939. *Black Workers and the New Unions.* Chapel Hill: University of North Carolina Press, 1939.
CBTU Convention Proceedings. 1972. CBTU Resolutions, Chicago, September 23–24. Rev. Addie and Rev. Claude Wyatt Papers, Box 103, Folder 8, Vivian G. Harsh Research Collection of the Chicago Public Library.

Center for Economic and Policy Research. 2013. *Slow Progress for Fast Food Workers*. Washington, DC: Schmitt, J. & Jones, J.

Center for Labor Research and Education. 2013. Fast Food, Poverty Wages: *The Public Cost of Low-Wage Jobs in the Fast-Food Industry*. Berkeley, CA: Allegreto, S.A., Doussard, M., Graham-Squire, D., Jacobs, K., Thompson, D. & Thompson, J.

Ehrenreich, Barbara. 2001. *Nickel and Dimed: On (Not) Getting By In America*. New York: Henry Holt and Company.

Flug, Michael. 1990. "Organized Labor and the Civil Rights Movement of the 1960s: The Case of the Maryland Freedom Union." *Labor History* 31(3): 322–46.

Foner, Philip S. 1981. *Organized Labor and the Black Worker, 1619–1981*. New York: International Publishers.

Foner, Philip. 1989. *Black Workers: A Documentary History from Colonial Times to the Present*. Philadelphia: Temple University Press.

Goluboff, Risa. 2005. *Let Economic Equality Take Care of Itself: The NAACP, Labor Litigation, and the Making of Civil Rights in the 1940s*. University of Virginia Law School Public Law and Legal Theory Working Paper Series, Paper 24.

Harris, William H. 1982. *The Harder We Run: Black Workers Since the Civil War*. New York: Oxford University Press.

Henry, Ben, and Allyson Fredericksen. 2013. *America's Changing Economy: Searching for Work That Pays in the New Low-Wage Job Market*. 2013 Job Gap Study. Alliance for a Just Society, December.

Hill, Herbert. 1961. *Racism within Organized Labor: A Report of Five Years of the AFL-CIO, 1955–1960*. Address delivered at NAACP Annual Meeting. New York, January 3.

Honey, Michael. 2000. *Black Workers Remember: An Oral History of Segregation, Unionism, and the Freedom Struggle*. Berkeley: University of California Press.

Hunter, Tera. 1998. *To 'Joy My Freedom: Southern Women's Lives and Labors after the Civil War*. Cambridge, MA: Harvard University Press.

Jacobson, Julius. 1968. *The Negro and the American Labor Movement*. New York: Anchor Books.

Johnston, Katie. 2014, "For those juggling multiple jobs, the workweek never ends." *Boston Globe,* December 5. Accessed from www.bostonglobe.com.

Kersten, Andrew. 2000. *Race, Jobs and the War: The FEPC in the Midwest, 1941–1946*. Urbana: University of Illinois Press.

Korstad, Robert. 2003. *Civil Rights Unionism: Tobacco Workers and the Struggle for Democracy in Mid-Twentieth-Century South*. Chapel Hill: University of North Carolina Press.

Levy, Peter. 1994. *The New Left and Labor in the 1960s*. Urbana: University of Illinois Press.

Liechtenstein, Nelson. 1982. *Labor's War at Home: The CIO in World War II*. New York: Cambridge University Press.

Lipsitz, George. 1994. *Rainbow at Midnight: Labor and Culture in the 1940s*. Urbana: University of Illinois Press.

MacLean, Nancy. 2004. "Achieving the Promise of the Civil Rights Act: Herbert Hill and the NAACP's Fight for Jobs and Justice," *Labor* 3 (2): 14–16.

Moody, Kim. 1988. *An Injury to All: The Decline of American Unionism.* New York: Verso Press.

National Employment Law Project. 2013. "Super-Sizing Public Costs: How Low Wages at Top Fast-Food Chains Leave Taxpayers Footing the Bill." Data Brief. October.

Nelson, Bruce. 2001. *Divided We Stand: American Workers and the Struggle for Black Equality.* Princeton, NJ: Princeton University Press.

Pfeffer, Paula. 1990. *A. Philip Randolph, Pioneer of the Civil Rights Movement.* Baton Rouge: Lousiana State University Press.

Proceedings of the Montgomery, Alabama Bus Boycott Conference. 1956, February 13. UPWA Papers, Box 373, Folder 6, Wisconsin Historical Society.

Schlosser, Eric. 2001. *Fast Food Nation: The Dark Side of the All American Meal.* New York: Houghton Mifflin Harcourt.

Schmitt, John, and Janelle Jones. 2013. "Slow Progress for Fast-Food Workers." Issue Brief. Center for Economic and Policy Research, August.

Shipleer, David. 2004. *The Working Poor: Invisible in America.* New York: Vintage Books.

Sugrue, Thomas. 1996. *The Origins of the Urban Crisis.* Princeton, NJ: Princeton University Press.

Thompson, Heather. 2001. *Whose Detroit? Politics, Labor and Race in a Modern American City.* Ithaca, NY: Cornell University Press.

Transcript of Civil Rights and Legislative Conference. September 23, 1963. UPWA Papers, Box 526, Wisconsin Historical Society.

US Bureau of Labor Statistics. 2012. "Labor Force Statistics from the Current Population Survey: 11. Employed persons by detailed occupation, sex, race and Hispanic or Latino Ethnicity." Alliance for a Just Society. 2013. *America's Changing Economy: The Job Gap.* Washington, DC: Gupta, Rahul.

White, Sarah, and Margaret Hollins. 1995. Interview with Michael Flug, Tape 5, Side 2, April 1995. Transcript, Sarah White Papers, Vivian G. Harsh Research Collection of the Chicago Public Library.

Wilson, William Julius. 1987. *The Truly Disadvantaged: The Inner City, the Underclass, and Public Policy.* Chicago: University of Chicago Press.

Wilson, William Julius. 1997. *When Work Disappears: The World of the New Urban Poor.* New York: Knopf.

"Women's Pride at Delta Pride." 1991. *CLUW News* 17, no. 1 (January–February). Tamiment Library, CLUW Papers, Box 230, Folder 18.

Zieger, Robert. 1995. *CIO, 1935–1955.* Chapel Hill: University of North Carolina Press.

Zook, Kristial Brent. 2006. *Black Women's Lives: Stories of Power and Pain.* New York: Nation Books.

Chapter 8

Affirming or Disconfirming America's Promise

Attitudes about Affirmative Action Among Black Americans and Black Immigrants

Anthony D. Greene, LaTasha Chaffin,
Maurice Mangum, and Jason E. Shelton

In the early 1960s, President John F. Kennedy is credited as saying that government contractors "take affirmative action to ensure that applicants are employed, and employees are treated during employment, without regard to their race, creed, color, or national origin" (UC-Irvine Office of Equal Opportunity and Diversity, 2010). This statement was issued as a part of Executive Order 10925, which was to affirm the government's commitment to equal opportunity for all qualified persons, and to take positive action to strengthen efforts to realize true equity. By 1965, during the midst of the civil rights movement, President Lyndon B. Johnson issued Executive Order 11246 prohibiting employment discrimination based on race, color, religion, and national origin by those organizations receiving federal contracts and subcontracts (e.g., affirmative action).

The intent of affirmative action was to balance the scales of inequality between whites and racial minorities, between men and women, and redress the patterns of discrimination against other disadvantaged and marginalized groups (i.e., the poor, military veterans, the elderly, and the disabled). Due to pressures by civil rights groups, federal legislation, and court rulings, affirmative action programs were implemented to address past racial discriminatory practices against racial minorities and women in educational institutions and among employers (Andre, Velasquez, Mazur, n.d.). These programs were met with wide-scale opposition. As such, practices such as hiring and admissions quotas were established to limit the number of women and racial minorities, thus creating a belief system that these groups were (are) unqualified, and more importantly, underserving.

Regardless of the efforts to undermine the use and purpose of affirmative action, evidence highlights why such policies remain not only beneficial but also necessary and relevant in the new millennium. For example, the National Asian and Pacific American Legal Consortium (n.d.) reported "that although white men make up only 48% of the college-educated workforce, they hold over 90% of the top jobs in the news media, 96% of CEO positions, 86% of law firm partnerships, and 85% of tenured college faculty." Practices of racial and gender exclusion are as prevalent today as it was fifty years ago.

Nonetheless, several groups continue to benefit from affirmative action, despite their perceived lack of support of such policies (see Wise 1998). Asians, Black immigrants (e.g., West Indian, African), and women, especially White women, have been some of the primary benefactors of affirmative action over the last fifty years (Cose 1997; Massey et al. 2007; Wise 1998). For instance, Black immigrant students, and children of Black immigrant parents, make up the majority of several elite universities' Black student populations (Massey et al. 2007).[1] The preferential recruitment and acceptance of Black immigrant students, and the subsequent lack of recruitment of African American students, at some of the nation's best universities have begun to raise questions about the role affirmative action policies in college enrollment.

Although the debate on its relevance is not a new issue, affirmative action remains a pertinent issue as we continue to see the growing academic and economic gap between not only Black and White Americans, but also between Black immigrant groups and African Americans (Pew Research Center 2013). African Americans, with a history of racial discrimination in housing, employment, and educational institutions, tend to support and advocate for affirmative action policies (Pew Research 2014). Although Black immigrants are not immune to racial discrimination, buttress for the dominant American ideology of success as the result of hard work would suggest there is a probability that Black immigrants oppose affirmative action policies.

THEORETICAL FRAMEWORK: INDIVIDUALISM VERSUS STRUCTURALISM

The history of American racism drives African Americans to support political policies that are designed to eradicate inequalities. Black immigrants, particularly first generation, are thought to adhere to the dominant American ideology of meritocracy (e.g., hard work equals success). As such, this suggests they are more likely to reject policies that are perceived to provide assistance to ensure success, rather than individuals being rewarded for individual effort and merit. We use two competing frameworks that can explain Blacks' support for policies such as affirmative action: structuralism and individualism. Blacks' support or rejection of the dominant ideology of hard work equals success is not uniform. African Americans and Black immigrant groups are extremely diverse culturally, socially, and politically. As such, political attitudes and support for social policies are as diverse as the population itself.

Individualism is the notion that people are responsible for their own socio-economic fate by virtue of their work ethic, talents, personal characteristics, and choices (Feagin 1975; Huber and Form, 1973; Hunt 1996, 2004; Kluegel and Smith, 1986). It also suggests that the American stratification system is open, impartial, and emphasizes fairness and the equality of opportunity (Reynolds and Xian 2014). Furthermore, ascriptive characteristics (e.g., race, gender) and other social characteristics (e.g., religious affiliation, sexual orientation) are not factors that limit an individual's opportunities. These attitudes can impact political and social beliefs. Experiences with racial discrimination, for many African Americans, do not foster beliefs that opportunity exist equally for all. As such, African Americans who reject the dominant ideology are more likely to support affirmative action policies. As for the first-generation Caribbeans, belief in the dominant American ideology as the primary factor for upward mobility may harbor more individualistic attitudes. Consequently, they would likely to reject policies like affirmative action. Similarly to other immigrant groups, achieving the American Dream is simply a process of hard work and a good education.

Structuralism contends that various patterns of power and prestige hinder opportunities for some people while simultaneously enriching them for others in American social institutions (Emerson & Smith 2000; Hunt 2007; Robinson 2009; Shelton and Emerson 2010; Shelton and Greene 2012). As such, racial discrimination is believed to inhibit groups' equal access to opportunities for upward mobility. Structural beliefs may foster stronger support for political policies designed to eradicate historical racial policies and increase access to opportunity and resources. African Americans traditionally harbor more structural attitudes (Hwang et al. 1998; Sigelman and Welch 1991), which suggests they are more likely to be in favor of policies that are used to deconstruct historical and disparities. Among Caribbeans, the second and third generation, recognize the salience of racial discrimination in the pursuit of upward mobility. As such, experiences with racial discrimination in the opportunity structure may influence their structural attitudes, thus increasing their views in the relevance of affirmative action policies.

LITERATURE REVIEW

Verba and Nie's (1987) finding on the importance of "group consciousness" and Dawson's (1994) conception of "linked fate" versus individual rational utility has been instrumental in understanding political behavior in the Black American community. These theories purport that many African Americans consider the "fate" of their collective racial group when making political decisions. It has been suggested that as African Americans' economic situation improves and discrimination declines, that group consciousness would supplant racial consciousness. However, Dawson (1994) found that even African Americans with higher socioeconomic status still felt connectedness and a sense of linked fate with the African American community. Dawson posits that African Americans are still affected by discrimination in society and despite individual achievement equate progress of their group with progress as individuals. According to this argument, as long as Black political interests align, which are different than White political interests, racial interests will outweigh class interests (Dawson, 1994).

Using OLS models, Chong and Kim (2006) found that, consistent with Dawson's (1994) findings, achieving higher economic status does not reduce African Americans' support for government efforts to address racial and ethnic inequality. However, Chong and Kim (2006) do find that the opposite is true for Hispanics and Asian Americans. An additional finding is that as Hispanics become more conservative and obtain higher education levels, their opposition to government intervention increases. Conservatism also had a modest yet similar effect on African Americans. Therefore it appears that, as Latino Americans do not have the same historical legacy in the United States that they may not share the same sense of "group consciousness" that African Americans experience with one another regardless of social and economic status. Chong and Kim (2006) also find that minorities who have conservative ideologies tend to fight less for the disenfranchised within their race.

Wilson's (1979) seminal work, *The Declining Significance of Race*, posited that African Americans in the 1970s and 1980s left the urban Black enclaves creating two distinct Black social worlds. These worlds, as Wilson states, "is becoming increasingly divided along class lines." In addition to the divisions in their social space (neighborhoods), upwardly mobile African Americans created new educational spaces (types of schools their children attend), political spaces (political affiliation and beliefs), and religious spaces (type of churches). As a consequence, these new lived experiences resulted in a shift in the attitudes about how racism and discrimination impacted opportunities for African Americans (Wilson 2012). Many successful African Americans began to maintain that individual effort (or lack thereof), not structural forms of discrimination, were the primary causes of African Americans' inability to become upwardly mobile.

Mangum (2008) hypothesized that African Americans with higher income, education, and social class would have greater support for affirmative action policies as they may benefit at a greater level than African Americans with lower socioeconomic status. He also hypothesized that as Black women tend to have a higher socioeconomic status than Black men, they may be more supportive of affirmative action policies as well. Additionally, he suggested that Blacks who perceive their socioeconomic status to be worse off than a previous time period and those that have experienced discrimination, especially older Blacks and southern Blacks with greater knowledge and/ or experience with Jim Crow, will be more supportive of affirmative action policies (Sigelman and Welch, 1991). Mangum (2008) found that while Blacks with higher education and those that considered themselves as having enjoying a higher class of social status were more supportive of affirmative action policies, contrary to Wilson's (1987) findings, more affluent higher income Blacks were less supportive of affirmative action. Mangum (2008) did find evidence to support that Blacks who were group conscientious were more supportive of affirmative action and Blacks that felt less warmly toward other racial groups were also more likely to support affirmative action policies. Blacks who felt how they were treated was due to their race and who perceived being discriminated against were also more likely to support affirmative action policies.

Despite the generally held belief of the "poor immigrant," many immigrant groups come to the United States with human capital traits (e.g., advanced degrees; professional job skills) that create a less complicated mode of incorporation into American society (Portes and Rumbaut 2001). Many Black immigrants, thus, are able to translate these human capital traits into middle-class social status. In fact, Black immigrants are disproportionately more middle class than African Americans (Kalmijn 1996; Tisdale 2015). For example, among African immigrants, 24 percent have attained at least a bachelor's degree (compared to 18% national average); 16 percent have earned a graduate degree (compared to 10% national average); and more than one-third work in white-collar professional jobs (Immigration Poverty Center 2012). Also, African immigrants are the best-educated new immigrants arriving to the United States (Massey, et al. 2007). With that said, several scholars investigate whether Black immigrants will forge social and political coalitions with their native-born counterparts (Rogers 2001/2004/2006; Watts-Smith 2014; Thorton 2013). In Watts-Smith (2014) analysis of the role of Black immigrants feelings of group consciousness (e.g., linked fate to African Americans) on political identities, they found that, for example, when Black immigrants encounter more discrimination, they are more supportive of political issues such as reparations for Blacks in the United States. Additionally, their sample of Black immigrants revealed social class status, education, and party affiliation (democrat) yielded more liberal attitudes on policy issues (e.g., Abortion; LGBT adoption). Accordingly, in this analysis, social class status, political party affiliation, and experiences with discrimination yield more liberal attitudes toward political issues in support for Blacks in the United States.

Blacks' political opinions are also influenced by social class (Patillo 2008/1999; Watts-Smith, Tate 1994), but the salience of racial discrimination complicates the discussion about support or rejection of affirmative action policies among Black-ethnic groups in the United States. On one hand, the growth of the Black American middle class and the strong presence of middle-class Black immigrants suggest some Blacks adhere to individualistic attitudes toward success and upward mobility (Hunt 2007; Wilson 2012), thereby likely to reject the usefulness of policies like affirmative action. On the other hand, there remains a disproportionate number of working-class/poor African Americans and a significant population of working-class/poor Black immigrants, who encounter racial discrimination regularly, thus cementing greater structural attitudes toward inequality (Shelton and Greene 2012; Sniderman and Piazza 2002; Waters 1999). Consequently, this segment of the Black population may support and advocate for affirmative action policies.

This investigation examines the variation of opinions on affirmative action among African Americans and Caribbeans. Given that there is no monolithic opinion on affirmative action among Blacks, we seek to understand the sources of division over a policy that is geared to include Blacks as beneficiaries. We anticipate that overall Caribbeans are not as supportive of affirmative action policies as African Americans. Moreover, we suspect that in general socioeconomic and demographic characteristics influence opinions on affirmative action policies. On the basis of prior empirical findings and theoretical underpinnings at the forefront of the current literature, we ask three questions to guide our analyses:

Q_1: Do Caribbeans support affirmative action policies similarly to African Americans?

Q_2: To what extent does socioeconomic factors influence opinions on affirmative action?

Q_3: Is support or opposition to affirmative action among African Americans and Caribbeans affected the same factors and do these factors influence both groups in the same manner?

Based on the following research questions, the proposed hypotheses will drive the analyses:

H_1: Caribbeans do not support affirmative action similarly to African Americans.

H_2: Blacks with higher levels of education and higher incomes are less likely to support affirmative action.

H$_3$: Blacks who are Democrats and experience more discrimination are more likely to support affirmative action.

METHODOLOGY

Utilizing data taken from the 2004 National Politics Study, we examine the opinions of African Americans (N = 697) and Caribbeans (N = 342) toward affirmative action. We also provide summary statistics and descriptive data on the 2004 National Politics sample (see Table 8.1). The opinions of Whites, Asians, Latinos, and members of other racial-ethnic groups are beyond the scope of the present study. We estimate one survey item from this multiracial data set as our dependent variable. The question asks respondents whether they believe affirmative action is a good thing, bad thing, or neither. Given there are only three response categories, we utilized ordered logit as the statistical method.

Predictor Variables

Each model incorporates featured predictor variables and control variables. There are five predictor variables that are of most theoretical importance in our investigation. *Hardworking Blacks* and *Hardworking Caribbeans* assess the extent to which respondents rate African Americans and Caribbeans from lazy to hardworking, respectively. *Racial Resentment* is a factor dimension that found that three of the following variables loaded onto one factor dimension (*Minorities to Blame, Bootstraps*, and *Blacks Deserve*). *Minorities to Blame* is the belief that if racial and ethnic minorities don't do well in life they have no one to blame but themselves; *Bootstraps* is the belief that if Irish, Italians, Jewish, and many other minorities overcame prejudice and worked their way up, and then Blacks should do the same without any special favors. *Blacks Deserve* is the belief that Blacks have gotten less than they deserve over the past few years. *Discrimination Blacks* and *Discrimination Caribbeans* assess the extent to which respondents believe that African Americans and Caribbeans experience discrimination from none at all to a lot of discrimination, respectively.

Table 8.1   Descriptive Statistics of Race-Ethnicity and Affirmative Action (N%)

	African Americans	Caribbeans
(1) A Bad Thing	77 (11%)	43 (12.6%)
(2) Neither Good Nor Bad	23 (3.3%)	11 (3.2%)
(3) A Good Thing	597 (85.7%)	288 (84.2%)
Mean	0.746	0.716
N	697 (100%)	342 (100%)

Source: National Politics Study (2004).

Control Variables

Age represents a continuous variable with a range from 17 to 100, with 45 as the average age. *Gender* was coded where 0 = male and 1 = female, where males are the reference category. *Education* was coded into a dichotomous variable where 0 = HS/some college (or less) and 1 = BA or more (e.g., MA, MBA, PhD). Sixty-two percent of the sample had some college or higher studies, whereas 38 percent of the overall sample possessed a BA and beyond. Family income was recoded into a dichotomous variable where 0 = working class and 1 = middle class or higher. South refers to whether the respondent lives in the south or not. Political ideology and party identification were also accounted for as the models include variables ascertaining whether respondents are a Liberal, Conservative, Democrat, and Republican.

We employ two different models as the Ideological Model is more nuanced than the Party Identification Model. The survey questioning in the ideology measure ranges from extremely conservative to extremely liberal, whereas the liberal or conservative measure in the Party Identification Model asks respondents to self-identify themselves as liberal, conservative, or other. Similarly in Ideological Model the survey measure asks respondents to identify themselves as Republican, Democrat Independent, other or no preference, whereas the Democrat or Republican measure only allows the options of Democrat, Republican, or other. The options presented to respondents in each model are varied enough we feel to warrant different modeling strategies. These effects are evident in the results as, for example, the ideology measure is significant in the Ideological Model, yet the liberal versus conservative measures are not in the Party Identification Model.

Dependent Variable

Affirmative action refers to any policy or law used to give qualified individuals equal access to employment, education, business, and contracting opportunities. *Affirmative Action* is measured using the following survey item: "Generally speaking, do you think affirmative action is a good thing or a bad thing?" The affirmative action variable was coded as -1 = "a bad thing," 0 = "neither good nor bad," 1 = "a good thing."

ANALYTICAL PLAN

We begin our analysis of the National Politics Study data (see Table 8.1) with descriptive statistics. The tests are conducted to explore preliminary differences between African Americans and Caribbeans. Secondly, and more importantly, we use ordered logit analyses to disaggregate what factors influence African Americans and Caribbeans' attitudes toward affirmative action. Ordered logit also allows for us to assess the role of socioeconomic factors, perceptions of their racial group, perceptions about discrimination and political ideology and beliefs. This is the appropriate statistical procedure for multivariate models assessing dichotomous dependent variables. Each of the two outcomes is separately regressed on a fully saturated model containing all specified predictors. Based on our coding scheme, odds ratios (OR) greater than 1 signal stronger support for affirmative action, while odds ratios less than 1 signal lesser support.

FINDINGS

Table 8.1 presents descriptive statistics for all variables. Overall, African Americans and Caribbeans report similar attitudes regarding affirmative action. When asked whether affirmative action is a bad thing, neither good nor bad, or a good thing they reported similar findings. For instance, 86 percent of African Americans and 84 percent of Caribbeans indicate that affirmative action is "a good thing." Conversely, only 11 percent of African Americans and 13 percent of Caribbeans indicate that affirmative action is a "bad thing." These findings suggest that despite ethnic variations, Blacks view and support affirmative action similarly.

Table 8.2 displays results from logistic regressions assessing whether affirmative action is a "good thing or bad thing." In the Ideology Model, African Americans and Caribbeans were in favor of affirmative action. Additionally, gender, educational attainment, ideology and party identification were significant predictors of whether affirmative action is a good or bad thing. Other significant variables included discrimination that Caribbeans experience (DiscC); and the factor variable (Min Blame, Bootstra & Deserve) that measures whether respondents feel that minorities have no one to blame but themselves if they don't do well in life; whether African Americans should overcome prejudice and work their way up like other ethnic minorities (e.g., Jewish); and whether respondents feel that African Americans have received less than they deserve.

Additionally, more women supported affirmative action than men; individuals with fewer years of education tended to support affirmative action than respondents with more years of education. As Conservatives and Republicans have been fundamentally opposed to regulation of businesses and organizations' employment decisions and university admissions through affirmative action, it follows that respondents with a more liberal ideology supported affirmative action and in terms of party identification, more

Table 8.2   Ordered Logit Analyses of Affirmative Action Ideological Model

	Affirmative Action B (S.E.)	
African Americans	**0.474****	(0.154)
Caribbeans	**0.476****	(0.189)
Age	–0.004	(0.0034)
Gender	**–0.311****	(0.108)
Education	**–0.083****	(0.024)
Family Income	0.002	(0.0000001)
South	0.088	(0.110)
Ideology	**0.137****	(0.063)
Party ID	**0.420****	(0.078)
Hardworking Blacks	–0.026	(0.042)
Hardworking Caribbeans	0.032	(0.045)
Discrimination Blacks	–0.011	(0.080)
Discrimination Caribbeans	**0.172****	(0.073)
Factor (Minorities to Blame, Bootstra, Deserve)	**–0.599****	(0.065)
Cut 1	–1.54	(0.363)
Cut 2	–1.36	(0.362)

**p < .05.

Democrats supported affirmative action than Republicans. Furthermore, the more Caribbeans experienced discrimination, the more they supported affirmative action.

There was a negative relationship between the factor variable (Min Blame, Bootstra & Deserve) and support for affirmative action. Therefore those respondents that believe that African Americans aren't solely to "blame" for their situation and disagree that success for African Americans is only a matter of them pulling themselves up by their bootstraps, generally support affirmative action. It follows that Caribbeans and African Americans are more favorable of affirmative action than their counterparts. However, African Americans are slightly more favorable of affirmative action than Caribbeans (see Figures 8.2, 8.4, & 8.5).

Table 8.3 displays results from the logistic regression assessing party identification and support for affirmative action. In the Party Identification Model, African Americans and Caribbeans were in favor of affirmative action. Additionally, gender, education, Republican, and Democrat (to a lesser level of significance) were all significant predictors of support/rejection of affirmative action. Similar to the Ideological Model, Caribbeans' experiencing discrimination was in favor of affirmative action. Ironically, this was not true for African Americans. Also, those respondents represented in the factor variable who generally supported African Americans tended to favor affirmative action.

Table 8.3 Ordered Logit Analyses of Affirmative Action Party Identification Model

	Affirmative Action B (S.E.)	
African Americans	**0.474****	(0.154)
Caribbeans	**0.480****	(0.189)
Age	−0.003	(0.004)
Gender	**−0.325****	(0.109)
Education	**−0.079****	(0.025)
Family Income	0.00000007	(0.0000001)
South	0.082	(0.111)
Liberal	0.184	(0.191)
Conservative	−0.69	(0.189)
Democrat	**0.230***	(0.130)
Republican	**−0.646****	(0.146)
Hardworking Blacks	−0.028	(0.042)
Hardworking Caribbeans	−0.031	(0.045)
Discrimination Blacks	−0.018	(0.080)
Discrimination Caribbeans	**0.177****	(0.073)
Factor (MinBlame, Bootstra, Deserve)	**−0.60****	(0.065)
Cut 1	−1.576	(0.408)
Cut 2	−1.397	(0.408)

**p < .05; *p < .10.

As with the Ideological Model, women supported affirmative action more than men; individuals with fewer years of education supported affirmative action more than those respondents with greater education; Democrats supported affirmative action (to a lesser significance) than Republicans (with a greater degree of significance) who were generally not supportive of affirmative action. When experiencing discrimination, Caribbeans are more likely to support affirmative action.

It was notable in this model that the measures of liberalism and conservatism were not significant, nor was region, age, or family income measures. Again, African Americans who believed they were discriminated against were not significant, yet Caribbeans' perception of discrimination impacted their support for affirmative action. Whether African Americans or Caribbeans perceived that their race-ethnicity was hardworking was not a significant factor in this model.

DISCUSSION

What is notable from the analysis is that both American-born and Caribbeans generally favor affirmative action policies (see Figures 8.1 and 8.2). Additionally, the mean support for affirmative action is only slightly higher

Anthony D. Greene et.al.

Affirmative Action Support by African Americans

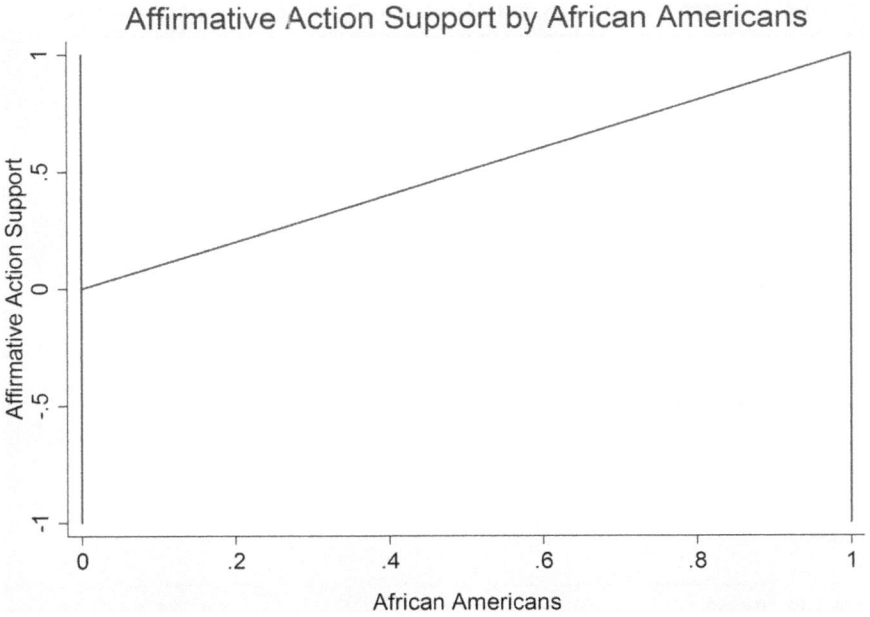

Figure 8.1   Affirmative Action Support by African Americans.

Affirmative Action Support by African Americans
0 = Non-African Americans 1 = African Americans

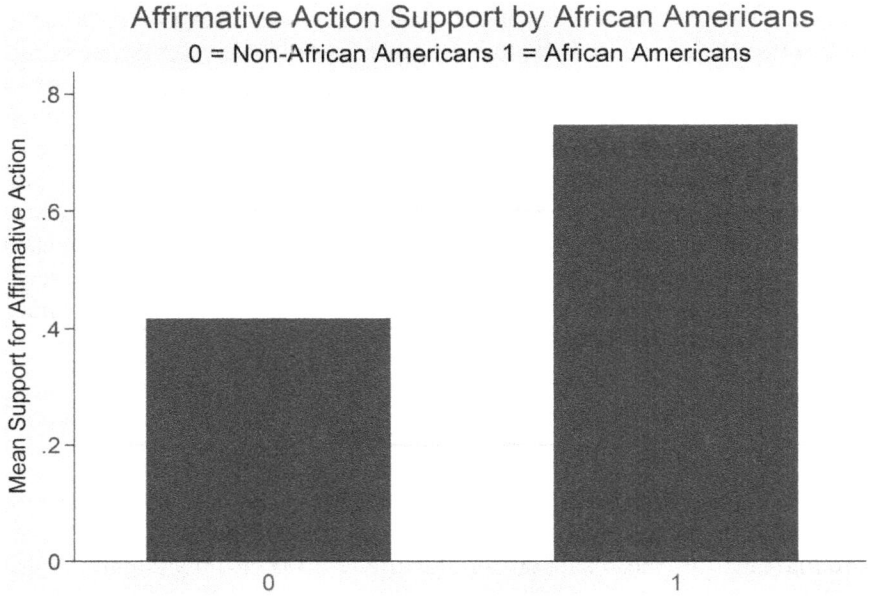

Figure 8.2   Affirmative Action Support by African Americans.

for African Americans than Caribbeans (see Figures 8.3 and 8.4). Therefore, theories that purport that Caribbeans do not support policies that promote equality in employment and admissions through affirmative action programs are not reflective in this analysis. In essence, Caribbeans that respond that affirmative action is "a good thing" or "neither good nor bad" is virtually indistinguishable from African Americans. However, Caribbeans that are not supportive of affirmative action respond that affirmative action is "a bad thing" at a slightly higher rate than African Americans (see Table 8.1).

When analyzing perceptions of discrimination, the respondents' view of whether their group was hardworking or lazy did not factor into whether or not African Americans or Caribbeans asserted that affirmative action was a good or bad thing. However, Caribbeans' perception of whether they faced discrimination as a result of their race or ethnicity had a significant impact on whether or not they supported affirmative action policies. Conversely, experiencing discrimination did not have the same significant influence on African Americans. This may be because African Americans have become anesthetized to discrimination in the United States, where this is a new experience for Caribbeans. Perceptions about minority group status do matter however for levels of support for affirmative action policies as the combined factor model however was largely significant. When respondents feel that minorities

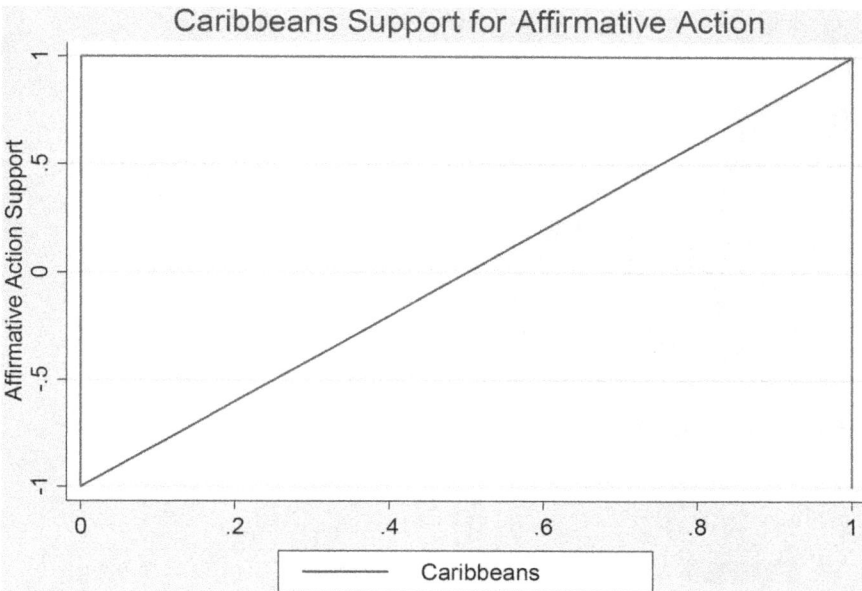

Figure 8.3 Affirmative Action Support by Caribbeans.

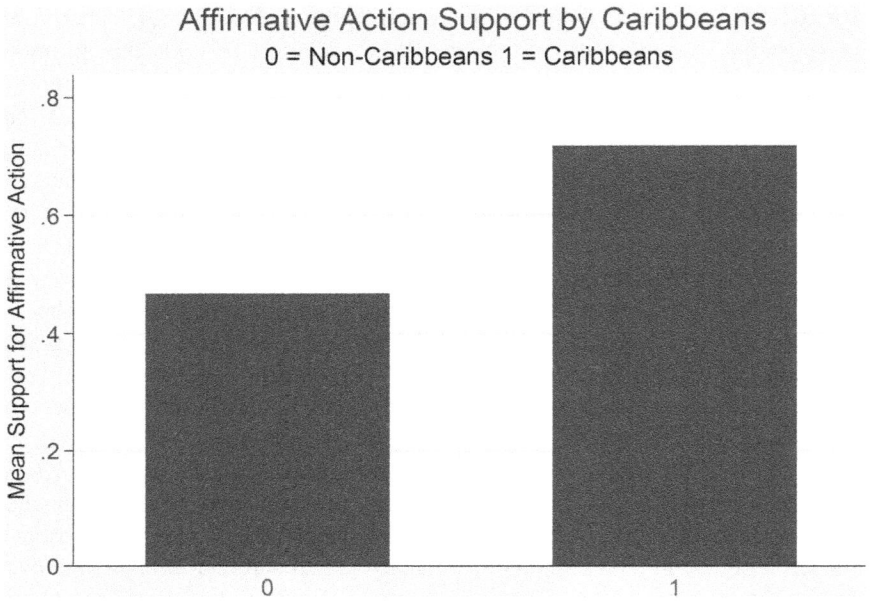

Figure 8.4   **Affirmative Action Support by Caribbeans.**

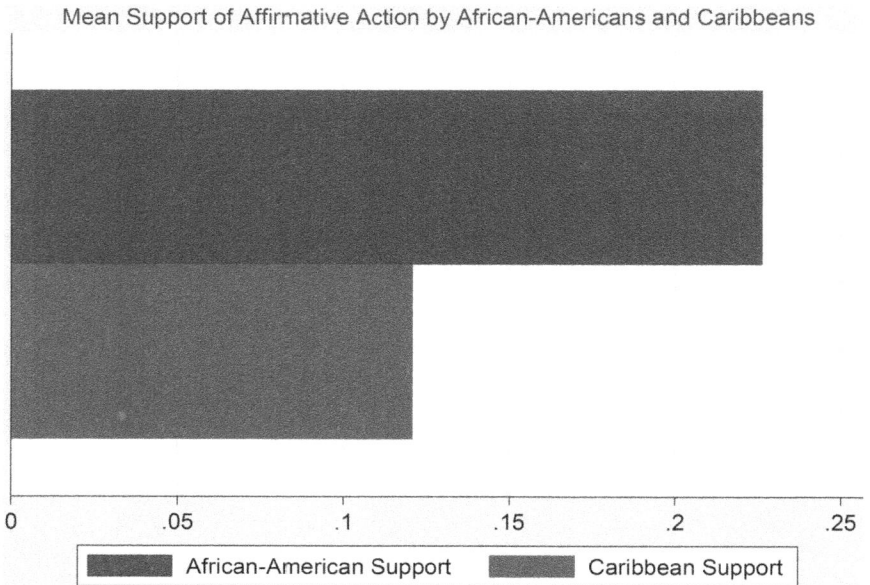

Figure 8.5   **Support of Affirmative Action by African Americans and Caribbeans.**

aren't solely to blame but themselves if they don't do well in life, that Blacks should not just have to overcome prejudice and work their way up like other ethnic minorities (e.g., Jewish), and assert that Blacks have gotten less than they deserve, they tend to support affirmative action.

Where respondents fell on the liberalism to conservatism scale mattered. Pursuant to party platform and ideals of liberalism, respondents who identified as more liberal and as Democrats, were more supportive of affirmative action policies. Conversely, self-identified Conservatives and Republicans were against regulation of businesses and educational institution through affirmative action programs. The ideological and political beliefs from conservatives are not surprising considering the efforts to eliminate affirmative action policies in enrollment practices in higher education (see *Fisher vs. University of Texas*).

Surprisingly, socioeconomic variables did not influence individuals' support for affirmative action. However, perceptions of discrimination and political preferences were influential. It might be expected that older African Americans may be more apt to be supportive of affirmative action, having connections or remembrance of the civil rights era, as opposed to younger African Americans who are deemed a part of a potentially post-racial society. Nonetheless, there was no significant relationship between age and respondents' perceptions. Family income also did not play a significant role in determining Blacks support for affirmative action. More affluent respondents that experienced discrimination had an awareness or sensibility of how Blacks were negatively perceived in society, and did not ascribe to these perceptions tended to support affirmative action. In this context, income status did not matter. Blacks residential location (living in the south or other regions) did not influence support for or against affirmative action. Despite region, race, regardless of being West Indian of Black American mattered more. Gender, not surprisingly, was a significant predictor of support for affirmative action. Women, who are the largest beneficiaries of affirmative action, were in strong support of these policies.

CONCLUSION

Since the advent of affirmative action, proponents have applauded its efforts to address institutional forms of racial discrimination in hiring practices and higher education enrollment patterns. Opponents, however, continue to argue that such policies are unnecessary and tend to benefit unqualified individuals. Although more than just a race-based policy, the debate often is divided along racial lines. A number of lawsuits have targeted the use of affirmative action in college admissions and hiring practices among some of the country's most elite institutions and corporations. Despite its intent to dismantle traditional and historical injustices, affirmative action policies continue to stir up debate over racial and gender equity. Scholars, politicians, lobbyist, and activists who contest affirmative action tend to argue that affirmative action is a policy designed to give unfair advantages to racial minorities, particularly Black Americans (Ayuda 2010; Lott 2014; Mott 2014). Most often the argument centers on the partial advantages given to unqualified/under-qualified Blacks in higher education admissions and job opportunities over more qualified Whites. Growing disapproval and changing attitudes over the past four decades has resulted in efforts to dismantle affirmative action policies or to dramatically overhaul the policy.

With undeniable increases of women in fields such as law, business, medicine (e.g., doctors), engineering, and college faculty since the implementation of affirmative action, Cose (1997) states, "there are at least six million women—the overwhelming majority of them White—who simply wouldn't have the jobs they have today, but for the inroads made by affirmative action." Additionally, Asian students have significantly benefited from affirmative action policies in college admissions in states such as California (Lott 2014; The Economist 2014). Evidence shows that Black immigrant groups (e.g., West Indians, Africans) are recruited into the country's most prestigious universities at higher rates than African Americans. The question we pose, and subsequently assessed, was whether or not Caribbeans are as supportive as African Americans.

As Waters (1999) and Rumbaut and Portes (2001) suggest, Black immigrant groups, particularly the first generation, adopt the dominant American ideology regarding success in the United States. They uncovered that similar to other immigrant groups, Black immigrants adhere to the belief that hard work equals success. As such, this would indicate that Black immigrants would not favor policies such as affirmative action. Additionally, with the enrollment patterns at elite universities that favor Black immigrant groups over African Americans (Cross 2011; Fontaine 2009; Massey et al. 2007; Peck 2012), one could deduce that although benefiting from affirmative action, Black immigrants are not in favor of such policies and credit their successes primarily on their merits. Conversely, there continues to be a steady decline in African American enrollment at America's most elite private and public universities (Millhiser 2013). As such, African Americans continue to be significant proponents of policies like affirmative action.

The following study finds, nonetheless, that African Americans and Caribbeans support for affirmative action is analogous. More importantly, encounters with discrimination boost the support for such policies, especially among Caribbeans. As such, these findings reveal the salience of race in the lived experience of Black ethnic groups, regardless of their nationality or ethnic origin. Waters (1999) indicates that West Indians who adopt more of an African American identity subscribe to the tenants of racism in America. In other words, West Indians who see themselves as "racially similar" to African Americans understand how race can, and often does, limit their opportunities, thereby become advocates for policies used to address racial inequalities. With ongoing pressures to eliminate affirmative action policies, it appears that African Americans and Caribbeans stand in solidarity in their advocacy for policies designed to right the wrongs of institutional racism.

LIMITATIONS OF STUDY

Although this investigation generates significant discussions regarding the political support for affirmation action among Blacks, the analysis is unable to investigate generational differences. Several scholars have identified how generational status impacts immigrant groups' ideologies on several factors (Greene and Shelton forthcoming; Kasinitz 1992; Kasinitz, Battle, and Miyares 2001; Rumbaut and Portes; Waldinger and Feliciano 2004; Waters 1999; Watts-Smith 2014). Future analysis should include an examination of the political ideologies of second- and third-generation Black immigrants, born in the United States. As Watts-Smith (2014) notes, "perhaps second-generation immigrants are more likely to recognize the importance of descriptive representation than first-generation immigrants because they have been socialized in the United States." Acknowledging the variation within and between Black immigrants' generational status would provide added value to the overall discussion of the similarities and differences among African Americans, Caribbeans, and other Black-ethnic groups in the twenty-first century.

NOTE

1. In this paper, the references to Black immigrants are specifically toward Blacks who either have parents from the West Indies, Central/South America, or Africa but were born in the United States or themself from the West Indies, Central/South America, or Africa.

BIBLIOGRAPHY

Andre, Claire, Manuel Velasquez, and Tim Mazur. (n.d.). "Affirmation Action: Twenty Five Years of Controversy." Accessed from http://www.scu.edu/ethics/publications/iie/v5n2/affirmative.html.

Ayuda, Tiffany. 2010. "How Affirmative Action Affects Asian Americans." Accessed from http://www.mochimag.com/article/how-affirmative-action-affects-asian-americans.

Butcher, Kristen F. 1994. "Black Immigrants in the United States: A Comparison with Native Blacks and Other Immigrants." *Industrial & Labor Relations Review* 47:265–84.

Chong, Dennis and Dukhong Kim. 2006. "The Experiences and Effects of Economic Status Among Racial Ethnic Minorities." *American Political Science Review* 100(3): 335–51.

Cose, Ellis. 1997. *Color-blind: Seeing Beyond Race in a Race-obsessed World.* New York: HarperCollins.

Cross, Lawrence. 2011. "Harvard has more Black Students than Ever, but are they African-American?" Retrieved from http://thegrio.com/2011/04/21/harvard-has-more-black-students-than-ever-but-are-they-african-american/.

Dawson, Michael 2001. *Black Visions: The Roots of Contemporary African American Political Ideologies.* Chicago, IL: University of Chicago Press.

Emerson, Michael O. and Christian Smith. 2000. *Divided by Faith: Evangelical Religion and the Problem of Race in America.* New York: Oxford University Press.

———. 1994. *Behind the Mule: Race and Class in African American Politics.* Princeton, NJ: Princeton University Press.

Feagin, Joe. 1975. *Subordinating the Poor.* Englewood Cliffs, NJ: Prentice Hall.

Feagin, Joe and Melvin Sikes. 1994. *Living with Racism: The Black Middle Class Experience.* Boston, MA: Beacon Press.

Foner, Nancy. 2001. *Islands in the City: West Indian Migration to New York.* University of California Press.

———. 1998. "West Indian Identity in the Diaspora: Comparative and Historical Perspectives." *Latin American Perspectives*, 25(3): 173–88.

———. 1987. "The Jamaicans: Race and Ethnicity among Migrants in New York." In *New Immigrants in New York*, edited by Nancy Foner, 195–217. New York: Columbia University Press.

Fontaine, Smokey. 2009. "Black Immigrants Overrepresented at Ivy League Schools." Accessed from http://newsone.com/214021/black-immigrants-overrepresented-at-ivy league-schools/.

Gurin, Patricia, Shirley Hatchett, and James Jackson. 1989. *Hope and Independence: Blacks' Response to Electoral and Party Politics.* New York: Russell Sage.

Huber, Joan and William H. Form. 1973. *Income and Ideology.* New York: The Free Press.

Hunt, Matthew O. 2007. "African American, Hispanic, and White Beliefs about Black/White Inequality, 1977–2004." *American Sociological Review* 72: 390–415.

Hunt, Matthew O. 2004. "Race/Ethnicity and Beliefs about Wealth and Poverty." *Social Science Quarterly* 85(3): 827–53.

Hsieh, Evelyn. 2009. "Following Obama, Students Define "Black" on Ivy League-Campuses." Accessed from http://www.huffingtonpost.com/evelyn-hsieh/barackobama has-broken-r_b_217965.html?ncid=dynaldusaolp00000255.

Hwang, Sean S., Kevin M. Fitzpatrick, and David Helms. 1998. "Class Difference in Racial Attitudes: A Divided Black America?" *Sociological Perspectives* 41(2): 367–380.

John, Arit. 2014. "Why the All-Ivy League Story Stirs Up Tensions Between African Immigrants and Black Americans." Accessed from http://news.yahoo.com/why-ivyleague-story-stirs-tensions-between-african-204556090.html.

Kalmijn, Matthijs. 1996. "The Socioeconomic Assimilation of Caribbean American Blacks." *Social Forces* 74(2): 911–30.

Kasinitz, Philip. 1992. *Caribbean New York: Black Immigrants and the Politics of Race*. Ithaca, NY: Cornell University Press.

Kasinitz, P, J. Battle, and I. Miyares. (2001). "Fade to Black: The Children of West Indian Immigrants in Southern Florida." In *Ethnicities:Children of Immigrants in America* edited by R. G. Rumbaut and A. Portes, 267–300. Berkeley, CA: University of California Press.

Kluegel, James R. and Eliot R. Smith. 1986. *Beliefs about Inequality*. New York: Aldine DeGruyter.

Leadership Conference on Civil Rights Education. (n.d.). Affirmative Action. Retrieved from http://www.civilrights.org/resources/civilrights101/affirmaction.html

Lott, Maxim. 2014. "Rejected Asian Students Sue Harvard Over Admissions that Favor Other Minorities." Accessed from http://www.foxnews.com/us/2014/11/18/rejected-asian-students-sue-harvard-over-admissions-that-favor-other-minorities.html

Mangum, Maruice. 2008. "Testing Competing Explanations of Black Opinion on Affirmative Action." *Policy Studies Journal.* 36 (3): 347–66.

Massey, Douglass, Mooney, Margarita, Torres, Kimberly C., Charles, Camille Z. 2007. "Black Immigrant and Black Native Attending Selective College and Universities in the United States." *American Journal of Education* 113: 243–71.

Millhiser, Ian. 2013. "Black Enrollment Falls 30 Percent at University of Michigan After Affirmative Action Ban." Accessed from http://think-progress.org/justice/2013/09/25/2677641/black-enrollment-falls-30 percent-at-university-of-michigan-after-affirmative-action-ban/

Mott, Maxim. 2014. "Rejected Asian Students Sue Harvard Over Admission that Favor Other Minorities." Accessed from https://storify.com/gmatcourse592/rejected-asian-students-sue-harvard-over-admission.

Peck, Patrice. 2012. "African-Americans vs. Black Immigrants: Do Institutions of Higher Learning Give Preference to Foreign Blacks?" Accessed from http://thegrio.com/2012/10/05/african-americans-vs-black-immigrants-do-institutions-of-higher-learning-give-preference-to-foreign-blacks/.

Pew Research Center. 2013. "Statistical Portrait of the U.S. Black Immigrant Population." Found in a Rising Share of the U.S. Black Population is Foreign Born.

Pew Research Center. 2014. "Public Strongly Backs Affirmative Action Programs on Campus." Accessed from http://www.pewresearch.org/fact-tank/2014/04/22/public-strongly-backs-affirmative-action-programs-on-campus/

Patillo, Mary. 2008. *Black on the Block: The Politics of Race and Class in the City*. University of Chicago Press.

———. 1999. "Black Picket Fences: Privilege and Peril among the Black Middle Class." University of Chicago Press.

Reynolds, Jeremy and He Xian. 2014. "Perceptions of Meritocracy in the Land of Opportunity." *Research in Social Stratification and Mobility*, 36: 121–37.

Rogers, Ruel R. 2006. *Afro-Caribbean Immigrants and the Politics of Incorporation:Ethnicity, Exception, or Exit.* New York: Cambridge University Press.

————. 2004. "Race-Based Coalitions among Minority Groups: Afro-Caribbean Immigrants and African Americans in New York City." *Urban Affairs Review* 39 (3): 283–317.

————. 2001. "Black Like Who? Afro-Caribbean Immigrants, African Americans, and the Politics of Group Identity." In *Islands in the City: West Indian Migration to New York* edited by Nancy, 163–92. Berkeley: University of California Press.

Shelton, Jason E. and Michael O. Emerson. 2012. *Blacks and Whites in Christian America.* New York: New York University Press.

Shelton, Jason E. and Anthony D. Greene. 2012. "Get Up, Get Out, and Git Sumthin': How Race and Class Influence African Americans' Attitudes about Inequality." *American Behavioral Scientist* 56 (11):1480–1507.

Sigelman, Lee and Susan Welch. 1991. *Black Americans' Views of Racial Inequality.* New York: Cambridge University Press.

Smith, Candis. 2014. *Black Mosaic: The Politics of Black Pan-Ethnic Diversity.* New York University Press.

Sniderman, Paul and Thomas Piazza. 2002. *Black Pride and Black Prejudice.* Princeton, NJ: Princeton University Press.

Tate, Katherine. 1994. *From Protest to Politics: The New Black Voters in American Elections.* Harvard University Press.

Thorton, Michael C., Robert J. Taylor, and Linda M. Chatters. 2013. "African American and Black Caribbean Mutual Feelings of Closeness: Findings from a National Probability Survey." *Journal of Black Studies* 44: 798–828.

Tisdale, Stacey. 2015. "Black Immigrants in U.S. Earning 30% more than U.S. Born Blacks: Different Economies Emerging for the 'Different Flavors of Black.'" Accessed from http://www.blackenterprise.com/money/black-immigrants-in-u-s-earning-30-more-than-u-s-born-blacks/

Verba, Sidney and Norma H. Nie. 1987. "Participation in America: Political Democracy and Social Equality." The University of Chicago Press.

Waldinger, Roger D. and Feliciano, Cynthia. 2004. "Will the New Second-generation Assimilate Downward? Segmented Assimilation Re-assessed." *Ethnic and Racial Studies* 27: 376–402.

Waters, Mary C. 1994. "Ethnic and Racial Identities of Second-generation Black Immigrants in New York City." *International Migration Review* 28: 795–820.

————. 1999. *Black Identities: West Indian Immigrant Dreams and American Realities.* Cambridge, MA: Harvard University Press.

Wilson, William. 2012. *The Declining Significance of Race: Black and the Changing American Institutions.* University of Chicago Press.

Wilson, William J. 1987. *The Truly Disadvantaged: The Inner City, the Underclass, and Public Policy.* The University of Chicago Press

Wise, Tim. 1998. "Is Sisterhood Conditional? White Women and the Rollback of Affirmative Action." *National Women's Studies Association Journal* 10: 3.

Chapter 9

An Obsolete People?

The Precarious Position of African Americans in the Twenty-First-Century Economy

Robert E. Weems, Jr.

The August 22, 2014, issue of the *Philadelphia Tribune* featured an essay by the syndicated African American columnist Jim Clingman with the provocative title "Black Americans Have Become Obsolete." In this work, Clingman provided a rather sobering assessment of the current status of African Americans in the US economy. He concluded by asserting that black people today have two choices, coalescence or obsolescence (Clingman 2014). This chapter, through additional analysis, will seek to ascertain whether Clingman's observations represent hyperbole or reality.

One of the major reference points in Jim Clingman's article is Sidney Wilhelm's 1970 book *Who Needs the Negro?* In the first chapter, entitled "Prospective for Black Obsolescence," Wilhelm discussed how the economic benefits for whites associated with slavery and its aftermath resulted in a consensus that "the Negro had to be tolerated." Yet, with rise of automation in the late twentieth century, black workers were transformed from being needed workers to being expendable and useless. Ominously, Wilhelm further declared that one of automation's consequences could be white America's promotion of "the Negro's dismissal" similar to "the elimination of the native Indian population less than a hundred years ago" (Wilhelm 1970, 2–3).

In the more than forty years after the publication of *Who Needs the Negro?* Wilhelm's allusions to overt genocide have not come to pass. No doubt, ongoing automation has negatively impacted the employment opportunities of minimally educated and unskilled black workers. Still, African American educational advances, during this same period, have significantly increased the number of skilled black workers and professionals. For instance, between 1970 and 2010 the number of African American men and women who had completed twelve or more years of schooling increased from 36 percent to 84.1 percent (Walton and Rockoff 2010, 555).

One concrete indication of ongoing significant black participation in the American workforce is African Americans' collective annual income or spending power. This figure has grown steadily since the late 1960s. In 1969, the noted African American marketing specialist D. Parke Gibson wrote a book entitled *The $30 Billion Negro* which reflected collective African American income at the time. Several years later, he wrote *$70 Billion in the Black* which conveyed what black spenders were contributing to the economy in 1978. An important milestone in terms of annual African American spending power was reached in 2013, when this amount crossed the trillion dollar threshold (Weems 1998 [Desegregating the Dollar], 75; Nielson 2013, 3).

Although aggregate income data suggests that African Americans have made significant economic progress since the 1960s, similar data, associated with wealth accumulation (the difference between *what we own* and *what we owe*), presents a far more sobering assessment. A February 2013 study published by the Institute on Assets and Social Policy (IASP) at Brandeis University indicates that, during the last generation, the wealth gap between blacks and whites has steadily increased. To quote from its "Key Findings" section, "tracing the same households over 25 years, the total wealth gap between white and African American families nearly triples, increasing from $85,000 in 1984 to $236,500 in 2009" (Shapiro, Meschede, and Osoro 2013, 1).

A major contributing factor to the growing wealth gap between blacks and whites was the collapse of real estate prices associated with the Great Recession of 2007–2009. As the IASP report noted, "homeownership is an even greater part of wealth composition for black families, amounting to 53 percent of wealth for blacks and 39 percent for whites." Consequently, "half the collective wealth of African-American families was stripped away during the Great Recession due to the dominant role of home equity in their wealth portfolios and the prevalence of predatory high-risk loans in communities of color" (Shapiro, Meschede, and Osoro 2013, 4).

Although African American incomes have increased over the last generation, long-standing (disproportionate) unemployment in the black community is another factor that has widened the wealth gap between blacks and whites. As the IASP noted, "unemployment affects all workers but . . . black workers are hit harder, more often, and for longer periods of time. With much lower beginning wealth levels and unequal returns on income, it is a greater challenge for African Americans to grow their family wealth holding in the face of worker instability" (Shapiro, Meschede, and Osoro 2013, 5).

Contemporary African Americans' diminished support of black-owned businesses is another factor that has retarded collective black wealth accumulation. The late twentieth and early twenty-first centuries have witnessed the decline and disappearance of many historic black-owned enterprises. In fact, the dichotomy between the rise in aggregate African American income and the concurrent decline and disappearance of black businesses suggests that African American consumerism, since the 1960s, may be better characterized as *spending weakness* instead of *spending power*. James Clingman, who discussed the concept of "spending weakness" in his 2001 book *Blackonomics: The Way to Psychological and Economic Freedom for African Americans,* appears to be the originator of this perspective (Clingman 2001, 103–105). Moreover, overwhelming African American consumer support of white business is a concrete way, in the context of Sidney Wilhelm's analysis, whereby African Americans continue to be perceived as "useful" to white financial interests.

One of the first mainstream industries to benefit mightily from increased African American spending was Hollywood. In fact, it is not hyperbole to suggest that black filmgoers helped Hollywood avert financial ruin during the early 1970s. Based upon the stunning financial success of Melvin Van Peeble's independently produced 1971 film *Sweet Sweetback's Badasss Song* (which cost $500,000 to make and reportedly grossed more than $10 million dollars in three months) and MGM's 1971 blockbuster *Shaft* (which cost $1.8 million and reportedly grossed more than $17 million within a year), Hollywood studios literally fell over themselves in a rush to get their share of the African American consumer market. By 1972, nearly 25 percent of Hollywood's projected future productions were black-oriented movies. By contrast, only 3 percent of Hollywood's 1970 releases were films primarily intended for African American audiences (Weems 1998, 82).

The term "blaxploitation" has been used to describe this aspect of African American history. While "blaxploitation" is not grammatically correct, it does convey the psychological manipulation of African American consumers during this period. For instance, as one contemporary pundit noted

> Right now, there is no question that the black audience, starved for years for films that see the world from a black point of view, is eating up just about anything that is slickly served. It is no accident that the most successful of the black films—both good and bad—invariably serve up heroes who "stick it to the Man." The intent of the new black films is not art but the commercial exploitation of the repressed anger of a relatively powerless community. (Weems 1998, 83)

Another group of white business owners who profited handsomely during the 1970s blaxploitation film era were theater owners. Out of the approximately 14,000 motion picture theaters during this period, fewer than twenty were owned and operated by African Americans (Weems 1998, 88). In the context of "the more things change, the more they stay the same," two decades later this situation had, in fact, gotten worse. By 1995, there were fewer than ten black-owned movie theaters in the United States. Consequently, blacks who wanted to view the spate of hip hop–influenced movies then being produced about "life in the hood" were in the ironic situation of having to do so at downtown and suburban cinema complexes (Weems 1998, 125).

Although *employed* African Americans have helped generate significant profits for white corporations since the late 1960s, the larger black community, again, still suffers from inordinately high unemployment rates. Moreover, with affirmative action initiatives coming under increasing attack, African American unemployment rates could rise even more (as educated black professionals may join their less educated fellow blacks in the jobless ranks).

In "Black People Have Become Obsolete," Jim Clingman posits that unless African Americans coalesce (come together economically) the group is headed toward serious trouble.

Unfortunately, as alluded to earlier, recent trends in this regard are not encouraging. Moreover, the history of black-owned insurance companies demonstrates that African Americans' lack of economic solidarity is long standing.

African American insurance companies, historically, have represented a cornerstone of black economic development. Evolving from a tradition of mutual aid dating back to Philadelphia's Free African Society founded in 1787, black-owned insurance companies have attempted to perpetuate economic and social cooperation among African Americans (see Weare 1973/1993; Henderson 1990; Weems 1996). Yet, as a disturbing prelude to the decline and disappearance of black insurers in recent decades, black consumer support of these enterprises, even during the height of American apartheid, left much to be desired.

During the first decades of the twentieth century, white insurance companies openly discriminated against African Americans. Some, like Prudential, refused to insure African Americans altogether. Others, like Metropolitan Life, offered insurance coverage to blacks but charged them higher premiums than their white counterparts. Moreover, Metropolitan Life and other white insurers who served black customers did not employ black agents (Weems 1996, 39–41).

Notwithstanding their unequal treatment in the early twentieth-century insurance marketplace, the majority of African American consumers still gave their business to white insurers during this period. Merah S. Stuart's 1940 classic study, *An Economic Detour: A History of Insurance in the Lives of American Negroes,* lamented this reality. According to Stuart's research, at the end of 1938, the weekly premium income of African American insurance companies was $248,910. Conversely, blacks paid white insurance companies $995,640 for coverage on a weekly basis (Stuart 1969/1940, 37). In apparent exasperation, Stuart, the historian of the National Negro Insurance Association, continued:

> Every one of the $248,910 paid into Negro companies is free to perform its natural function of helping to create employment to which the qualified among the group that spends it are eligible. Every one of the $995,640 paid by Negroes into white companies, as soon as paid over the line, becomes earmarked for discrimination against the group that spends it; and the employment these dollars help to create is forbidden fruit to the sons and daughters of those who each week unthoughtfully pay this price to keep the doors of opportunity closed against their own. (Stuart 1969/1940, 37–38)

Notwithstanding Merah S. Stuart's pessimism during the early 1940s, as the decade progressed, the fortunes of black insurers dramatically improved. In his 1962 study of African American insurance companies during the period of 1930–1960, David Abner identified the decade of 1940–1950 as being especially profitable for black insurers. Between 1940 and 1950, "insurance in force grew in the Negro companies at an annual rate three times that of the industry: 13.9 vs. 4.4 per cent." Similarly, "total income received by the Negro companies during the 1940–1950 decade increased at an average rate three times that of the industry: 13.4 vs. 4.4 per cent." Moreover, "the average annual rate of growth in total admitted assets was more than twice as high in the Negro companies than in the industry during the 1940–1950 decade: 15.9 vs. 6.7 per cent." Finally, "during the 1940–1950 decade, policy reserves grew in Negro companies at an average annual rate more than twice that of the industry: 14.5 vs. 6.1 per cent" (Stuart 1969/1940, 227–228). In sum, during the 1940s, African American insurance companies outperformed their white counterparts in several key areas.

There appeared to be a direct correlation between internal African American migration during World War II to take war-related jobs and the improved profitability of black insurance companies. As an assessment of African American participation in the US economy from 1860 to 1960 noted, between 1941 and 1945 "the number of Negro skilled and semiskilled men doubled." Similarly, African American women benefited financially because "large numbers shifted from farms and domestic service to other types of personal services, to factories, and to clerical jobs." Moreover, "the postwar years showed continued advances in most regards" (Hayes 1962, 1364).

White insurance companies, perhaps surprised by their black counterparts' strong performance during the 1940s, began to reevaluate the African American consumer market during the 1950s. Moreover, in a situation dripping with irony, the historic discrimination practiced by Prudential, Metropolitan Life, and other white insurers against blacks actually helped them to generate new business in the African American community. Because African Americans had previously been denied equitable insurance coverage with industry giants, it quickly became a status symbol among blacks to possess a nondiscriminatory policy from a mainstream insurance company (Weems 1996, 102–103).

Besides profiting from previous discrimination, companies such as Prudential and Metropolitan Life increased their market share in the African American community by recruiting top agents from black insurance companies. Similar to how Major League baseball teams secured the best talent from the old Negro Leagues, insurance industry giants, with promises of financial rewards, were able to secure a talented cadre of trained black insurance agents (Weems 1996, 103).

David Abner's research provides additional verification of white insurers' successful quest to reach the increasingly important Negro market. For instance, between 1943 and 1957, the number of white companies that insured African Americans nearly doubled from 55 to 104 (Abner 1962, 229–230). Moreover, this contributed to a significant profitability shift during the 1950s. Unlike the 1940s, the average annual growth of mainstream insurance companies' insurance in force during the decade of 1950–1960 "was almost twice that of the Negro companies: 9.6 vs. 5.3 per cent." Likewise, during the 1950s, the broad-based industry's figures for total income "averaged an annual rate more than one and one-half times as great as that of the Negro companies: 7.3 vs. 4.9 percent" (Abner 1962, 227).

The Chicago Metropolitan Assurance Company provides a pertinent case study as to how black insurers responded to this increased competition from their white counterparts. At its January 20, 1964, annual meeting, President George S. Harris squarely addressed the issue of employee defections:

> From this moment on, let no one among us look upon this company as some sort of stepping stone, a kind of training ground for some other job somewhere else. I understand that this is the attitude of certain white companies, who are willing to let us go to the expense of training and preparing personnel, and they take them when we have completed this training. Look not at your company as a minor league outfit, where ambitious people prepare for the major leagues. Remember, we are Negroes and any insurance company that employs more than 500 people should not be considered minor league in our eyesight. (Chicago Metropolitan Mutual Assurance Company 1964)

Besides appeals to racial pride and unity, Chicago Metropolitan and other black insurers sought to counteract growing competition from industry giants by seeking white clients. For example, Chicago Metropolitan's Board of Directors passed a November 22, 1961, resolution that stated "it would be a future policy of the company to employ competent persons in Agency and Office Administration without regard to race, creed, or color" (Chicago Metropolitan Mutual Assurance Company 1961). Chicago Met subsequently interviewed several whites for positions in the company's agency department (Moman 1986; Mr. Moman, who served in a variety of administrative capacities within the company, coordinated the writing of a brief company history in 1977). This attempt at racial integration, however, proved fruitless. While some of Chicago Metropolitan's black agents gladly defected to white-owned companies, white insurance agents were not similarly attracted to employment with this black firm (Moman 1986).

Other black insurers, besides Chicago Metropolitan, were similarly concerned with expanding their client base. In fact, the 1963 convention of the National Insurance Association (NIA), the trade association of the black-owned insurance industry, focused upon the issue of attracting white personnel. North Carolina Mutual's William A. Clement, the NIA's newly elected president, contended that unless black companies were successful in recruiting, selecting, training, and supervising other ethnic groups, "we will be limited in penetrating the total market" (NIA 1963, 4–5). Still, despite Clement's exhortations, black companies were subsequently unable to attract white employees and clients. Thus, by 1967, NIA companies were forced to conclude that their future operations would be dictated by ongoing de facto, if not de jure, racial exclusion (NIA 1967, 3).

The last decades of the twentieth century were extremely difficult for black-owned insurance companies. Trapped in the unenviable position of being unable to expand their client base, while simultaneously seeing white competitors secure more and more black policyholders, an increasing number of black insurers disappeared from the landscape of American business. From 1962 to 1992, the number of African American insurers dropped from fifty to twenty-three, a 54 percent decrease (Brimmer 1993, 147). Moreover, those that remained saw a significant decline in their assets and premium income relative to the mainstream insurance industry.

Between the years 1962 and 1992, the increase in black insurance companies' total assets lagged far behind similar figures for the industry at large. In 1962, the total assets of the top fifteen black insurers stood at $303 million. By 1992, the total assets of the top fifteen African American firms had risen to $711 million (Brimmer 1993, 309; *Black Enterprise* June 1993, 151). Nevertheless, figures for the entire US insurance industry make these black gains appear extremely miniscule, if not irrelevant. In 1962, all insurance firms owned admitted assets valued at $133 billion. By 1992, the total assets of US life insurance companies stood at over $1.6 *trillion dollars*. Thus, while African American insurers' total assets represented 0.23 percent of all US life insurance assets in 1962, this percentage dwindled to 0.05 by 1992 (Brimmer 1993, 309; *1993 Life Insurance Fact Book Update,* 46).

Between the years 1962 and 1992, the increase in black insurers' premium income also lagged far behind similar figures for the industry at large. In 1962, the top fifteen African American insurance companies received $71 million in premium income. Thirty years later, the top fifteen African American insurance companies collected $159 million. On the other hand, in 1962, all US life insurance companies received $19 billion in premium income. Thirty years later, this figure had risen to $282 billion (Brimmer 1993, 318; *Black Enterprise* June 1993, 151; *1993 Life Insurance Fact Book,* 36). Once again, a wide discrepancy existed between the black insurers' premium income increase over time and that of the industry as a whole. While the premium income of African American insurance companies grew by *124 percent* between 1962 and 1992, the premium income of all US companies increased by *1,385 percent.*

Since the mid- to late twentieth-century African American insurance companies experienced an absolute decline in their number, along with a relative decline in total assets and premium income; thus it should not be surprising that these firms also experienced significant staff reductions. At the end of 1977, America's then thirty-nine black-owned insurance companies employed 7,834 individuals. At the end of 1988, America's then thirty-one black-owned insurance companies employed 5,088 individuals (*Black Enterprise* June 1979, 173; *Black Enterprise* June 1989, 291). During the 1980s, the number of black-owned insurance companies declined by *7.9 percent* (39 to 31). Yet, during this decade, the number of persons employed by black-owned insurance companies declined by *35 percent* (7,834 to 5,088).

The 1990s featured an even steeper decline in both the number of African American insurance companies and the number of individuals employed by these enterprises. On December 31, 1988, America's thirty-one African American insurers employed 5,088 individuals. Ten years later, on December 31, 1998, America's ten black-owned insurance companies employed 1,801 personnel (*Black Enterprise* June 1989, 291; *Black Enterprise* June 1999, 220). Consequently, during the 1990s, the number of black-owned insurance companies declined by *68 percent* (31 to 10). Similarly, during this decade, the number of persons employed by black-owned insurance companies declined by *65 percent* (5,088 to 1,801).

While many Americans celebrated the coming of a new millennium, the early twenty-first century witnessed a continuation of the black insurance industry's accelerated decline. At the end of 1998, America's ten remaining black-owned insurance companies employed 1,801 individuals. Four years later, at the end of 2002, America's ten black-owned insurers employed 925 personnel (*Black Enterprise* June 1999, 220; *Black Enterprise* June 2003,

209). Thus, between 1998 and 2002, the number of persons employed by African American insurance companies declined by *49 percent* (1801 to 925). Astonishingly, the number of persons employed by black insurance companies declined by *99 percent* (7,834 to 925) during the twenty-five year period from 1977 to 2002. Moreover, it must be noted that many of these lost jobs were professional, not minimum-wage, positions.

Other data further indicates that, by the turn of the twenty-first century, African American insurance companies had become all but irrelevant. Between 1996 and 2002, African Americans spent *$52.2 billion* on insurance, but during the same period, the combined premium income of the top ten black insurance companies was *$1.1 billion.* Put another way, in this same period, slightly less than *$0.02* of every dollar that African Americans spent on insurance was with black-owned firms (Target Market News, *Buying Power,* 1996–2002; *Black Enterprise,* "Black Insurance Companies," June 1997, 196; *Black Enterprise,* "Black Insurance Companies," June 1998, 187; *Black Enterprise,* "Black Insurance Companies," June 1999, 216; *Black Enterprise,* "Black Insurance Companies," June 2000, 206; *Black Enterprise,* "Black Insurance Companies," June 2001, 206; *Black Enterprise,* "Financial Services Overview," June 2002, 220; *Black Enterprise,* "B.E. Financial Services Overview," June 2003, 200).

The years 2003–2004 were especially brutal for the African American insurance industry. During those years, the number of profitable black insurers dropped from ten to five and the remaining five black firms had a collective premium income of *$326.6 million.* Conversely, according to the authoritative *Target Market News,* African American consumers in 2003 and 2004 spent *$32.2 billion* on insurance. Viewed proportionately, approximately *$0.01* of every dollar spent by African Americans went to black insurers in 2003 and 2004 (Target Market News, *Buying Power,* 2003; Target Market News, *Expenditures,* 2004; *Black Enterprise,* "B.E. Financial Services," June 2004, 204; *Black Enterprise,* "B.E. Financial Services," June 2005, 186). Currently, the two remaining black insurance companies, North Carolina Mutual and Atlanta Life, attract a microscopic portion of black consumer spending.

Economy of scale is an important business principle that has also contributed to the decline and disappearance of black insurance companies. Just as supermarkets can offer more economical prices than mom and pop grocers, large mainstream insurance companies can offer cost-conscious African American consumers more economical coverage than smaller black-owned insurance companies.

On the surface, it may appear that late twentieth- and early twenty-first-century African American consumers are being better served by white insurance companies (with their lower prices) than by historic black insurers.

However, a closer look at the previous relationship between black insurance companies and black consumers dispels such a notion. The history of the African American insurance industry reveals these firms' long-time commitment to reinvesting a significant proportion of their premium income back into the black community (primarily in the form of mortgage loans) (see Weare 1973/1993; Henderson 1990; Weems 1996; these three primary works related to African American insurance companies reveal the firms' historic commitment to black community economic development). As these companies have declined and disappeared, there has been a simultaneous decline and disappearance of the money these firms have designated for community reinvestment. Thus, the seeming parallel deterioration of African American insurance companies and urban black America's infrastructure appears far from coincidental. Significantly, while white-owned insurers readily take African Americans' premium payments, they appear far less enthusiastic about investing in African American enclaves.

African American consumers' current relationship with mainstream insurance companies and other non-black corporate entities, while not necessarily a manifestation of obsolescence, clearly raises the issue of economic self-destruction. Although individual African Americans possess more consumer goods than ever before, one would be hard-pressed to see where increased African American consumer spending has improved the infrastructure and ambiance of black neighborhoods across the country. Black consumers, who now travel to white-controlled downtown and suburban shopping malls to purchase white-produced products, enhance the economic base of these outside areas to the detriment of their own enclaves.

During this time of rampant African American financial illiteracy, history may provide a useful antidote and model. The Detroit Housewives' League, which grew from fifty to 10,000 members between 1930 and 1935, represents an important historical attempt to use black dollars to enhance African American community development. To join the League, African American women pledged to support black businesses, buy black-produced products, and patronize black professionals. Considering that African American women generally coordinated their families' spending patterns, the League sought to mobilize this power toward community development. Darlene Clark Hine's 1994 essay "The Housewives' League of Detroit: Black Women and Economic Nationalism," aptly referred to this strategy as "economic housekeeping" (Hine, Brown and Terborg-Penn, 1993, 584–586; Hine 1994, 133).

Despite the existence of such historical models as the Detroit Housewives League, the financial illiteracy exhibited by African American consumers in recent decades may be too much to overcome. The growing decline and disappearance of black-owned banks represents another manifestation of this sobering reality.

Between 1987 and 2015, the number of African American banks in the United States declined from 91 to 24 (Elstein 2015). Many of these casualties came in the wake of the 2008 US financial crisis (which disproportionately hurt African Americans). Harlem's Carver Federal, the largest remaining black bank in America, survived only through an infusion of outside capital. As a March 22, 2015, article on Carver Federal noted,

> The federal government agreed to rescue the bank, and Goldman Sachs, Morgan Stanley, Prudential Financial, Citigroup and others injected $55 million in cash. But existing Carver shareholders, many of them Harlem residents who for decades had turned to the bank for mortgages or savings accounts, were left with just a 2% stake. *The nation's largest African-American run bank was no longer African-American owned.* (emphasis added) (Elstein 2015)

Considering that contemporary African Americans possess a financial infrastructure that is greatly diminished (insurance companies) and increasingly controlled by others (banks), today's blacks, as characterized by James Clingman, possess an extremely tenuous position in the American economy. Moreover, in the wake of another possible economic downturn, the few remnants of African American community economic development may be totally destroyed.

In the end, African Americans find themselves in an economic conundrum. On the one hand, African American spending patterns for the past several decades, which overwhelmingly supported white-owned businesses, helped forestall being viewed as economically obsolete by whites. Yet, these same spending patterns resulted in an inexplicable voluntary disavowal of community economic development.

Robert H. Kinzer's and Edward Sagarin's 1950 classic *The Negro in American Business: The Conflict Between Separatism and Integration* provides an important historical perspective to recent African American economic history. According to Kinzer and Sagarin, the primary dilemma the mid-twentieth-century African American faced was how to "facilitate the breakdown of segregation, [and] enhance the possibilities of integration and infiltration, without endangering what little economic advantages [linked with racial segregation] he now enjoys" (Kinzer and Sagarin 1950, 23).

Kinzer and Sagarin, citing various distinct European ethnic neighborhoods that existed at the time, perceptively argued that separatism and integration were not necessarily mutually exclusive propositions. For instance, all of these enclaves featured merchants who spoke the language of their particular group, catered to the tastes of their ethnic brethren, and extolled the notion of homeland-linked solidarity (Kinzer and Sagarin 1950, 151–152). Yet, at the same time, "side by side with their small restricted economy, the immigrants and their American-born children have taken their place as part of the general economic picture" (Kinzer and Sagarin 1950, 152).

Kinzer and Sagarin's analysis included the important disclaimer that "the heritage of slavery on the one hand, and the comparative ease of biological distinctiveness of the Negro, on the other, have made integration [for African Americans] extremely difficult" (Kinzer and Sagarin 1950, 153). Considering this reality, Kinzer and Sagarin insinuated that it truly made sense for African Americans to maintain their business infrastructure since custom and law inhibited their quest for more opportunities in the larger economy. Moreover, Kinzer and Sagarin argued that, because separatism and integration were not mutually exclusive options for blacks, "*it would be impossible at this time to suggest that either pathway be abandoned, because there would be an obvious sacrifice that the Negro people can ill afford to make*" (Kinzer and Sagarin 1950, 169, emphasis added).

In 2016, the wisdom of Kinzer and Sagarin's observations appear crystal clear. In a capitalist society that gives top priority to ownership, contemporary African Americans have become an extremely vulnerable population without a substantive economic base. Whether this definitively leads to the black obsolescence that James Clingman discussed, only time will tell.

BIBLIOGRAPHY

1993 Life Insurance Fact Book Update.

Abner, David. 1962. *Some Aspects of the Growth of Negro Legal Reserve Insurance Companies, 1930–1960.* Thesis, Indiana University, 229–230.

Black Enterprise. 1979, 1989, 1993, 1999, 2003. June.

———. "B.E. Financial Services Overview." 2003–2005. *Black Enterprise.* June.

———. "Black Insurance Companies." 1997–2001. *Black Enterprise.* June.

———. "Financial Services Overview." 2002. *Black Enterprise.* June.

Brimmer, Andrew. 1966. "The Negro in the National Economy." In *The American Negro Reference Book,* edited by John P. Davis. Englewood Cliffs, NJ: Prentice-Hall.

Brimmer, Andrew. 1993. *Economic Cost of Discrimination Against Black Americans.* Brimmer & Company.

Chicago Metropolitan Mutual Assurance Company. 1961. Minutes, Board of Directors Meeting, November 22.

———. 1964. Minutes, Annual Meeting, January 20.

Clingman, James. 2001. *Blackonomics: The Way to Psychological and Economic Freedom for African Americans.* Los Angeles: Milligan Books.

———. 2014. "Black Americans Have Become Obsolete." *Philadelphia Tribune,* August 22.

Elstein, Aaron. 2015. "Saving Carver Federal, NY's Last Black Bank." *Crain's New York Business,* March 22.

Gibson, D. Parke. 1961. *The 30 Billion Dollar Negro.* New York: Macmillan Publishers.

Hayes, Marion. 1962. "A Century of Change: Negroes in the U.S. Economy, 1860–1960." *Monthly Labor Review* 85: 1364.

Henderson, Alexa B. 1990. *Atlanta Life Insurance Company: Guardian of Black Economic Dignity.* Tuscaloosa: University of Alabama Press.

Hine, Darlene Clark. 1994. *Hine Sight: Black Women and the Re-construction of American History.* Bloomington: Indiana University Press.

Hine, Darlene Clark, Elsa Barkley Brown and Rosalyn Terborg-Penn (editors). 1993. *Black Women in America: A Historical Encyclopedia.* Brooklyn: Carlson.

Kinzer, Robert H., and Edward Sagarin. 1950. *The Negro in American Business: The Conflict Between Separatism and Integration.* New York: Greenberg Publishers.

Moman, Jesse L. 1986. Interview, February 11.

National Insurance Association. 1963. *Pilot* (Post-Convention Issue) 11: 4–5. Archives of the National Insurance Association, Amistad Research Center, New Orleans.

———. 1967. *Pilot* 16 (August): 3. Archives of the National Insurance Association, Amistad Research Center, New Orleans.

Shapiro, Thomas, Tatjana Meschede, and Sam Osoro. 2013. *The Roots of the Widening Racial Wealth Gap: Explaining the Black-White Economic Divide.* Research and Policy Brief, Institute on Assets and Social Policy, Brandeis University, February.

Stuart, Merah S. 1969. *An Economic Detour: A History of insurance in the Lives of American Negroes.* College Park, MD: McGrath Publishing; originally published in 1940.

Target Market News. 1996–2002. *The Buying Power of Black America.*

———. 2003. *The Buying Power of Black America, 2003.*

———. 2004. *Expenditures for All Black Households for 2004.*

Walton, Gary M. and Hugh Rockoff. 2010. *History of the American Economy,* 12th ed. Mason, OH: South-Western, Cengage Learning, 555.

Weare, Walter B. 1973. *Black Business in the New South: A Social History of the North Carolina Mutual Life Insurance Company.* Urbana: University of Illinois Press; reprinted in 1993 by Duke University Press.

Weems, Robert E., Jr. 1996. *Black Business in the Black Metropolis: The Chicago Metropolitan Assurance Company, 1925–1985.* Bloomington: Indiana University Press.

———. 1998. *Desegregating the Dollar: African American Consumerism in the Twentieth Century.* New York: New York University Press.

———. 2013. *Resilient, Receptive and Relevant: The African American Consumer, 2013 Report.* New York: Nielson.

Wilhem, Sidney. 1970. *Who Needs The Negro.* Cambridge, MA: Schenkman, 2–3.

Chapter 10

New (Pan)-Africanism or Neoliberal Globalization?

Introducing Nigeria's Africapitalism and South Africa's Ubuntu Business

Rita Kiki Edozie

In January 2016, the Tony Elumelu Entrepreneurship Program (TEEP) announced the selection of the first of 1,000 African entrepreneurs to train, fund, mentor, and empower the next generation of African and African diaspora entrepreneurs. The program's longer-term, ten-year goal is to help grow 10,000 start-ups from across the continent and create one million new jobs and $10 billion in annual revenues for Africa's economy (Nsehe 2015). TEEP is a program of Nigerian billionaire Tony Elumelu's Tony Elumelu Foundation (TEF). The nonprofit organization characterizes itself as a Pan-African organization that is premised on a concept coined by the billionaire entrepreneur as Africapitalism. In a related event, addressing an East African Community (EAC) forum, South African parliamentarian Mfuniselwa Bhengu proposed Ubuntu economics to positively contribute to the socioeconomic development of postcolonial Africa while also providing the continent with a competitive edge in world markets. In this regard, according to Bhengu, the EAC would need to integrate the innovative African practices and processes anchored in the Ubuntu value system to achieve competitive parity as opposed to competitive advantage for African economies in a global era (Moyo 2015).

Both incidents are expressions of new and alternative ideas and practices we refer to as the key theme for the current essay, a Pan-African political economy. While addressing East Africa's EAC, Bhengu rightly asked important questions about African affairs: Has the time not come for Africa to have her own Pan-African economic philosophy? Why must the continent separate economics from culture as mainstream global economic approaches do? Does neoliberalism fail in African settings because it is not embedded within African culture? These questions echo the Pan-Africanist orientation of founding Pan-Africanist Kwame Nkrumah's thesis about African unity being achieved—through economics as its strategy, and politics as its goal (Marah 2007). Already conscious of the way that colonial balkanization would lead to the neocolonialism of Africa, given that most of Africa's new nations were too small to avert economic dependency in a then emergent global economy, Nkrumah advocated the creation of the Organization of African Unity (now the African Union) with specific economic goals to break the pattern of economic exploitation established through colonialism.

The African Union underscores the role of culture for African economic integration: "Culture, heritage and a common identity and destiny will be the center of African strategies to facilitate for a Pan-African approach and the African Renaissance" (AU Agenda 2063). The African Union's 2015 Agenda 2063 supports the notion that Nkrumah's Pan-African economic dream is alive and well in the politics of contemporary Africa. Agenda 2063 engages the Pan-Africanist economic worldview a little differently from Nkrumah's 1960s decolonizing arena. In today's global era, Pan-Africanist orientations operate in a "glocalized" (local-global) African world. That is to say, according to Andrew Heron, in an era of globalization, local place is a particular moment in the spatialized networks of social relations whereby it functions as an entrance to the global processes that encircle the world.

Too few accounts of the contemporary African international economy draw from George Padmore's classic 1955 book, *Pan-Africanism or Communism*, where Pan-Africanism is presented as a political-economic development model for independent Africa in contrast to both communism and capitalism. Since the AU's establishment in 2002 at the helm of neoliberal global capitalism and again since 2009's post-neoliberal era, African Renaissance discourses have led to the resurgence of Pan-Africanist discourses in the continent that present a blueprint for Africa's difference in the international political economy. These discourses and practices are increasingly Africentric, nationalistic, and Pan-Africanist. And while engaging with more entrenched hegemonic IPE structures of neoliberalism and their poststructuralist discontents, new Pan-Africanist political economies present greater African ownership, nuance, agency, alterity, and distinctive cultural context for engaging the African international political economy.

Despite the fact that Africapitalism is shrouded in controversy and criticism, especially from Africa's Leftist scholarly class, Tony Elumelu invokes his self-styled characterization of capitalist practice in Africa as one route to seek answers to Bhengu's questions. Elumelu uses Africapitalism to target strategic economic sectors for investment such as agriculture, power, health care, and finance to create broad-based capitalist development that will provide inclusive opportunities for the greatest number of Africans. In this regard, Africapitalism relies on African values—self-determination, collectivism, and social value—to distinguish Africapitalism from neoliberal global capitalism's individualistic and competitive values. According to Elumelu, "No one can develop Africa better than Africans, and I believe foreign investors would be happier to have local investors there too" (Elumelu 2014).

Similarly, Ubuntu business and economics is presented as an African worldview that also seeks answers to Africa's economic dilemmas. The Ubuntu worldview—that South African–derived view that values communitarian humanity—seems to have had much longer universal acceptance as an African philosophy. The late Nelson Mandela once stated that Ubuntu did not mean that people should not enrich themselves, but rather if they were going to do so, they should do so in order to enable the community around them to be able to improve (Nelson Madiba Mandela). As it is manifested through African collectivist humanistic acts, such as codependency and collective reliance, in society, politics and the economy, Ubuntu economics and business principles invoke African culture as a key driver of change in the continent.

Are Africapitalism and Ubuntu economics, national-level forces in Africa, pushing for African integration? How are we to understand their ideological trajectories, and which of these are likely to enhance, contradict, undermine, or complicate the Pan-African project? Can their agenda be made to dovetail with the Pan-African project? What are the interests of this emergent class in the Pan-African project and its capacities to exploit the enlarged economic space? Africapitalist and Ubuntu economic business actors at the national levels in Nigeria and South Africa present intriguing case studies to evaluate prospects for rethinking Pan-Africanism at the national level. The business practices of Tony Elumelu and economist Mfuniselwa Bhengu are examined in this essay as glocalized, national-level Pan-Africanist philosophies and practices. K. K. Dompere's *Africentricity and African Nationalism: Philosophy and Ideology for Africa's Complete Emancipation* (Dompere 1992) has linked African nationalist and Africentric practices in local, community, and national domains as part and parcel of the broader Pan-Africanist rubric. None, he argued, would necessarily be radically antisystemic, antiglobalist, or anticapitalist per se; rather these Pan-Africanist philosophies would broaden the scope and demographics of political control while privileging homegrown economic solutions.

The current essay engages Minister Bhengu's questions by examining Africapitalism and Ubuntu as manifestations of new Pan-African international political economies emerging from Nigerian and South African postnational arenas. Whereas in the 1960s, Padmore asked Africans to choose between Pan-Africanism or communism, in today's economy we explore Africa's choices between new instances of Pan-Africanism and neoliberal globalization. Africapitalism self-defines itself as a vehicle that may rein in runaway globalization. It also claims to engage corporate social responsibility

(CSR) and creating shared value (CSV) as vehicles that direct the private sector to contribute to the societal benefits of the development of Africa. Ubuntu economic philosophies, for their part, assert a value system based on an African philosophy that we are one moral universe and that a shared moral sense makes humans recognize their duty to each other. Ubuntu presumes core elements that are contrasted against Western capitalism such as communalism versus individualism, cooperative systems versus hierarchical institutions, and the underscoring of humanness in social interaction versus viewing humans as mere economic objects like consumers, laborers, or owners.

The current essay is excerpted from a larger manuscript study that supports the prospect of Pan-Africanism as a route to Africa's "Third Way" engagement in the international political economy.

DIFFERENCE, CULTURE, AND IDENTITY
IN AFRICAN DEVELOPMENT

Solutions to African economic challenges in a global economy must come from African conditions, contexts, and solutions. China and Latin America, who tend to bypass either liberal mercantilist or structuralist approaches to IPE, have discovered that custom, self-reliant approaches drawn from several or alternative models tend to be best practice approaches for the current global economy. Custom political-economic approaches draw from local, national, and regional contexts. Africans will not be different. While the late Patrick Chabal's 2009 book, *The Politics of Suffering and Smiling in Africa*, may sometimes appear reductionist in presenting African peoples as victims of their leaders, their cultures, and neocolonial, global institutions and actors, it does direct us to a more appropriate combination of culture and political economy that represents an important theory for alternative and custom political-economic models. In his book, Chabal claims that our political thinking about African politics ought to be driven by the need to address the immediacy of everyday life and death. How do people define who they are? Where do they belong? What do they believe? How do they struggle to survive and improve their lives?

Chabal's approach represents a cultural political economy approach in its attention to the humanistic aspects of politics and economics underscoring the importance of simultaneously engaging core issues of economic growth, inequality, poverty, and development through the larger prism of their impact on people's lives and their perspectives in global context. Chabal's questions remind us of the need to examine the crucial significance of economic life in determining differential life chances of Africans across the globe, and they urge a rejection in the belief that orthodox models of economic life can fully capture the nature and dynamics of the African economy. New cultural political economy studies illustrate ways that various aspects of culture in its broad sense of the meanings that we give social life and material objects, as well as the concrete practices that it enables and depends on for its sustenance (Best and Paterson 2010). They underscore the importance of the everyday historical, social, and cultural intersections of international political economy.

Cultural international political economists who belong to the "decolonial" school are providing alternative theories of international relations and international political economy. These theorists integrate culture into IPE analyses while also maintaining a structuralist analysis and a powerful critique of the project of modernity that underlies much development thinking for the purpose of realistically understanding Africa's marginal positionality in the world. Enrique Dussel, for example, puts forth transmodernity theory as a multiplicity of responses to Euro-centered modernity; it is a modernity that is derived from the subaltern cultures and epistemic locations of formerly colonized people around the world. This "critical thinking from the margins" is an epistemic theoretical intervention that challenges the mythology of the West as the only epistemic site from which the rest of the world can be described, conceptualized, and ranked (Mignolo 2000; Grosfoguel 2011; Ndlovu-Gatsheni 2013).

Decolonialist thinkers critically relate discourses and histories about Africa's colonial legacies to formulate a recalibrated thesis about the underdevelopment of Africa by integrating notions of African subjectivity and identity into African political-economic practices and discourse. Such discourses differ from mainstream development discourses, which are seen to "otherize" Africans, deeming them incomplete without the achievement of development, for example. In this regard, development policies thereby become technologies of subjectivation using the cultural, social, and economic production of Africa as interventions (Escobar 1995). However, decolonialist cultural political economy appropriately brings back in the African philosophy rendition of the African development debate, which had at its core the tension between tradition and modernity. Messay Kebede outlined a critical problem, stating that while ethno-philosophy thinks that the rehabilitation of African traditions conditions the drive to successful modernization, especially after the disparaging discourse of colonialism, professional philosophy is of the opinion that success depends on the exchange of the traditional culture with modern ideas and institutions. Illustrating the importance of culture, identity, and subjectivity analyses of the African international political economy, Kebede contends that theories accounting for the underdevelopment of Africa too often attribute the African lag to colonialism and neocolonialism or to African inadequacies or to both (Kebede 1999).

What is needed instead is the reality that Africa's development has occurred as an alternative modernity. Indeed with independence beginning in the late 1950s and 1960s, the path to modernity for Africa was always an alternative one compared to the Western route. Alternative modernity's paths differ from Western modernity's paths to capitalism. African economic routes to modernity have occurred in very distinctive paths—anticolonial, dependent capitalism and resistance, late developmentalism, state industrialization and political-economic experimentalism. Afromodernity informs a third route to modernity in Africa. Michael Hanchard describes Afromodernity as a particular understanding of modernity and modern subjectivity; among people of African descent, including continental Africans, it consists of the selective incorporation of technological discoveries and institutions of the modern West, though within the cultural and political practices of African-derived peoples to create a form of relatively autonomous modernity that is distinctive from its Western counterparts. Afromodernity is not simply a mimicry of Western modernity, but it is an innovation upon its precepts, forces, and features. According to Hanchard, Afromodernity is the antithesis of Western modernity based on a supranational formulation of people of African descent that is not territorially demarcated, but based on shared anti-Western experiences, alternative IPE networks, and a critique of underdevelopment (Hanchard 1999).

Afromodernity in Africa is why the critical decolonial economists avoid a framework whereby development is seen as exogenous to Africa, something that inserts communities into a global capitalist hegemonic agenda, stripping local people's agency, power of imagination, and ability to design their own futures (Asabere-Ameyaw et al. 2014). In their book, *Indigenist African Development*, authors Akwasi Asabere-Ameyaw, Jophus Anamuah-Mensah, George Sefa Dei, and Kolawole Raheem attempt to think creatively about African development that is promoted through local creativity, imagination, ingenuity, and resourcefulness of local peoples (Asabere-Ameyaw et al. 2014). The authors use "indigenist" development to define and conceptualize development as a process and practice informed by home grown, locally informed, and locally driven initiatives to satisfy local needs and aspirations (Asabere-Ameyaw et al. 2014, 3). Asabere-Ameyaw et al.'s thesis provides further motivation for an IPE approach to Africa that critiques existing paradigms that ignore current processes of change in Africa today and regional, national, and local African contexts. Their cultural political economy frameworks serve to resuscitate the theory of Pan-African economics as an international political economy that engages with the popular prescriptions of continental public policies.

In today's quasi-post-neoliberal era (post-2007 global recession), mainstream scholars are celebratory of Africa's engagement in the global economy. Steven Radelet's *Emerging Africa: How 17 Countries Are Leading the Way* (Center for Global Development 2010) captures what has become commonplace in its characterization of the "emerging Africa" thesis in which he categorizes much of the continent as an "emerging market" region. Examining seven African countries, Radelet describes the positive economic outlook of Africa and attributes success to the rise of democracy, strong economic management, the end of the debt crisis, the introduction of new technologies, and the emergence of a new generation of African leaders. However, while apparently adopting the same trope of "emerging Africa" in his book's title *Emerging Africa: How the Global Economy's 'Last Frontier' Can Prosper and Matter,* Kingsley Chiedu Moghalu challenges the "Africa as the new frontier" mantra in globalization.

Moghalu's book challenges the notion that as the West lies battered by financial crisis, Africa offers limitless opportunities for wealth creation in the march of globalization. It asks important questions about African agency and self-definition in the global economy "What is Africa to today's Africans? Are its economies truly on the rise?" Here we can turn to the ways that Africans are reshaping Pan-Africanism for some answers.

THE PAN-AFRICAN GLOBAL POLITICAL ECONOMY

The cultural or constructivist turn in international political economy opens up the prospect for a new way for Africa to engage with the global economy through the principles of Pan-Africanism. Over its more than century-long evolution, Pan-Africanism has been driven by different actors responding to a number of external pressures. From its origins as movement for the assertion of the humanity of the people of African origin it now appears as a movement both for collective self-reliance and the new regionalism (Mkandawire 2008). In 1956, seething from his breakaway from the Communist International where he accused the communists of not understanding Africans' need to achieve "mental" liberation as well as materialist freedom, George Padmore wrote his book *Pan-Africanism or Communism?* (Padmore 1956). According to Padmore, communism was a grave danger to Pan-Africanism and the anticolonial struggle. While Adi (2013) acknowledged the interlocution of Pan-Africanism and communism, Padmore's real thesis was to present the values of Pan-Africanism over an emergent capitalism for decolonizing African nations. Ujaama, in Julius Nyerere's words, was "neither capitalism nor socialism"; this would be Africa's distinctiveness.

In 2016, Pan-Africanist economic thought is still considered in formulating a road-map for Africa's alternative engagement in the international political economy of African development and progress. Dr. Carl Lopes, the Cape

Verde economist who is also the secretary general of the UN's Economic Commission for Africa, has written of the role that Pan-Africanism could play in Africa's economy. For Lopes, today's Pan-Africanism reflects Africa's conscious need for not only political independence, regional integration, and the improvements of its living standards but also for throwing of the shackles of economic bondage and democratic stagnation that had seen it reverse the short-lived prosperity of the independence era. This means devising a new economic positioning and new forms of partnership in which Africa, as an equal partner, would negotiate with the rest of the world, with fierce defense of its own defined priorities. Without losing the key elements of unity, cultural heritage, and freedom, the reinterpretation of Pan-Africanism in the form of an African Renaissance is very relevant. It is a new phase that requires popular participation and mobilization of the African people behind the goals of structural transformation and improved governance. Indeed, Africa's Renaissance can only be complete when the African voice will be heard and taken into account. Lopez' call for a reinterpretation of the African international political economy to resuscitate and reconfigure Pan-Africanism to affect radical change for the continent, reflects Africa's modern Third Way.

Former South African president Thabo Mbeki has also recently employed the notion of a political and economic Pan-African Renaissance based on "Afromodernity"—modernity combined with African heritage to expand the Ubuntu worldview beyond politics and restorative justice to South African business, socioeconomics, and corporate governance. Africapitalism is also promoted as a Pan-African Afromodernity, as it provides a template for developing national economies differently from the modern West, as well as also achieving its best results when its principles are applied on a continental scale with the promotion of inter-African trade as a means to stimulating manufacture, skills mobility, and the economic development of Africans.

Pan-Africanism is an Afromodernity that deals with power and interest, their dynamics in the international arena, in international political forums, and in the international political economy (Lumumba-Kasongo 1994, 109). The late Kwame Nkrumah defined Pan-African unity as a nationalist survival shield that protected Africans from the vulnerability of neocolonialism. Pan-Africanist economics was used to attain an African command over all vital African economic decisions, which was essential for the achievement of economic reconstruction against underdevelopment for the continent (Green and Seidman 1966). In relation to development thereby, Pan-Africanism would find ways to exercise control over international economic forces that foster the continued process of underdevelopment and alternatively redirect economic policy for Africans toward African goals and contexts (Cohen and Daniel 1981, 251).

Pan-Africanism and African perspectives on African development have historically been intertwined into a single ideology since the 1960s by the OAU/AU (Africa Institute of South Africa. 2002). The pillars of Pan-Africanist political economy have been collective self-reliance and self-sustaining development, African-owned economic growth, and equitable redistribution (Maloka 2002); "delinking and auto-centricity," intraregionalism, and equitable globalism (Africa Institute of South Africa 2002). Newer theories of Pan-African IPE demonstrate the philosophy's national and community orientation in a global era. Malawian economist Thandika Mkandawire has argued that there is a need for a continued democratizing of Pan-Africanism if it is to be useful for reintegrating African regional economies. In light of the hostility of neoliberalism to regionalism and continued tensions between intracontinental economic objectives and extra-African economic objectives, Mkandawire suggests Pan-Africanism's contemporary utility is its ability to awaken African civil societies and capitalist classes in Africa for whom Pan-Africanism can provide a vehicle for a new national growth agenda (Mkandawire 2008).

In determining the importance of national anchoring and national-level democracy to the success or failure of Pan-Africanism, Mkandawire considers whether there are forces at the national level that are pushing for African integration and whether it is worth expending effort on political mobilization and lobbying of those forces and institutions. What are the ideological trajectories of the old and new social groups in this respect? And which of these are likely to enhance, contradict, undermine, or complicate the Pan-African project? Can their agenda be made to dovetail with the Pan-African project? Among other national actors—political parties, intellectuals, intelligentsia, social movements, and NGOs—Mkandawire identifies African capitalist classes as good prospects for such a role. He argues that in order to answer his questions one will have to identify the key actors at the national level and identify their real and perceived economic interests. With what he refers to as indigenous capitalists, Mkandawire acknowledges that there has been an ideological sea change in Africa, with much greater acceptance of the private sector and markets than there was in the 1960s and 1970s. But what is not yet clear are the interests of this emergent class in the Pan-African project and its capacity to exploit the enlarged economic space. Africapitalist and Ubuntu economic business actors at the national levels in Nigeria and South Africa present intriguing case studies to evaluate Mkandawire's predictions about Pan-Africanism at the national level (Mkandawire 2008).

Opoku (2004) assessed Pan-Africanist grassroots activism using the All-African Trade Union Federation (AATUF) as a case study. While Opoku's findings concluded that the AATUF was a failure of Pan-Africanism, more than ten years have passed since the publication of his book, and there may be alternative truths and realities on the ground. One may examine Africapitalism and Ubuntu economics as new instances of Pan-Africanist politics that engage in and benefit from the international political economy in ways that transcend underdevelopmentalism and its attendant colonial structures. They offer prospects for bringing alternative routes to modernization in Africa. In considering whether the Pan-African agenda can reverse underdevelopmentalism, dispossession, and dependence, more investigation into current contexts will be needed Pan-Africanism has a long history of resisting underdevelopment, and looking at the long-term effects of current, multiple new manifestations of it will be needed before concluding, as Opoku's study does, that it is a failure.

Pan-Africanist theory approaches the African economic experience through the prism of struggle and agency. On the one hand, agency is used to present a critical review of existing paradigms which have failed to capture an analytical framework that does justice to the processes of social change that are actually taking place today (Chabal 2009). On the other hand, presenting Africapitalism and Ubuntu economics as resuscitations of glocal Pan-Africanisms underscores that we are still fighting colonial legacies and struggling to infuse African histories, agencies, and identities into economics and to foster an alternate modernity rooted in African contexts. Through agency, business classes may represent a link between democracy and the market, both of which privilege an analysis of African social forces in terms of the empowered individual endowed with social, political, and economic rights (Chabal 2009).

AFRICAPITALISM AND UBUNTU ECONOMIC PHILOSOPHIES

Africapitalism and Ubuntu economic philosophies and practices currently have their most dynamic presences as progenitors that are providing societal engagement and impact as socioeconomic and political organizations based in Lagos, Nigeria and in Johannesburg, South Africa. Their Pan-Africanist efforts are manifest in their inclination and capacity to (1) refocus Africa's place in the global political economy; (2) direct Africa's private and non-profit sectors to contribute to benefit African communities; and (3) cultivate an Afri-consciousness among African communities that will guide Africa's Renaissance.

Nigeria and South Africa provide examples of both Africapitalist and Ubunto practices. Nigerian entrepreneur Tony Elumelu represents the Africapitalist approach, which he first expressed in a 2013 white paper. As CEO of the UBA Group for thirteen years, where he was responsible for using the bank to build a reputation for innovation and the democratization of banking services across Africa and for providing services to more than ten million customers worldwide. In launching first the Tony Elumelu Foundation, the *Africapitalist* magazine, and more recently the Africapitalist Institute, Elumelu sought to prove that the African private sector (over the international capitalist sector) could itself be the primary generator of economic development. Local content generation, for example, is an important policy objective of the *Africapitalist*. Elumelu believes that local content policies promote the quantum of composite value added to Nigeria through utilization of Nigerian resources and services in Nigerian industry that will result in the development of Nigerian business capability and employment (Balouga 2012).

On the other hand, Ubunto finds its chief advocates in South Africa, where it has long and deep roots. Entrepreneurs Michael Tellinger, Reuel Khoza, and Mfuniselwa J. Bhengu are cultural entrepreneurs who draw from Ubuntu philosophies to apply it to the economy. Their key objective for Ubuntu economics is to use it as a platform to serve people, and not for people to serve the economy. Like Africapitalism, according to Mfuniselwa J. Bhengu, the aim for Ubuntu economics is to create an African self-understanding, in economic terms. These business leaders are Afromodern Afroglobalists who are engaging in a national public-private sector dialogue within their respective economies.

Nigeria's Tony Elumelu and South Africa's Reuel Khoza represent an awakening of a burgeoning transnational capitalist class, middle class, and business sector in Africa. Both seek to initiate national, regional, and international public-private sector dialogues on African political economies and to interject African visions, values, and philosophies into business practices and economic outcomes.

Both Africapitalism and Ubuntu economics reveal the cultural dimensions of African political economy. They have emerged in the historical context of the continent's ongoing global marginalization, dependency, and underdevelopment in a global system that has been defined by a set of attitudes, norms, and ideas that have facilitated the continent's peripheralization and marginal status. Africapitalism and Ubuntu economics offer prospects for the examination of Pan-African economic philosophies and political-economic practices in consideration of their potential to positively transform Africa in a globalized world.

Each philosophy offers a viable development agenda for Africa for the twenty-first century. Africapitalism speaks to the reality that Africans are both resilient and ingenious in the management of their circumstances as many succeed in ways that are not obvious or that remain invisible to the unintended observer. As is the case with contemporary models of cultural capitalism and their emphasis on "business social responsibility" and other everyday habits and practices in economics, Africapitalism's value is also in its promotion of capitalism in Africa as an Afromodernity—a way to demonstrate how Africans can indeed be successful at capitalism.

Ubuntu economics, on the other hand, may speak more directly to the underside of capitalist failures in directly addressing the depth of suffering endured by the millions of desperately poor people in the continent who have no access to the emergent capitalistic benefits that are essential to life in Africa. Ubuntu economics may also be seen to belong to a genre of new economics once considered socialist, including new practices of resource-based economics, gift economies, and everyday livelihood issues. In this regard, one may consider Ubuntu economics in relation to classical African socialist practices such as Julius Nyerere's Ujaama. On the other hand, however, Reuel Khoza argues that the challenge for Ubuntu economics is not to abolish capitalism but to humanize it through a determination to act ethically toward others.

Elumelu and Khoza are representative of many others in Africa's new, burgeoning capitalist class, their organizations and institutions, and their leadership discourses. Each business sector's leadership in fostering an Afri-conscious ideology and worldview in business and economic practices serves to refocus Africa's political-economic practices in the world. Moreover, while both philosophies and practices may seem to be very different—one based in capitalism (Africapitalism) and the other in socialism (Ubuntu economics)—we see now both converge as new and alternative, third expressions of Pan-African economics in the African continent and that further may inform renewed bases for continental regional integration. It may be the case, nonetheless, that in accordance with the main ideological objective of Pan-Africanism, both Africapitalism and Ubuntu economics' goal to "Africanize" an economy that is currently still extraverted and externalized is a shared and thus requisite objective on its own terms.

This common goal of "Africanizing" the economy means that Africapitalism and Ubuntu economics may not be mutually exclusive in the way that capitalism and socialism are usually understood in liberal and structuralist frameworks. In a cultural political economy framework, both may exist simultaneously in concert or together in reinforcing each other in generating agency among Africans in their strive to control their own economic determinations. Both reveal how, in a global era, Pan-Africanism can be a potent ideology in the continent's local, regional, and national as well as global arenas.

CONCLUSION

A preliminary observation of both new Pan-Africanist economic philosophies reveals to us that Africapitalism and Ubuntu philosophies are contemporary manifestations of alternate modernity that are integrating cultural dimensions of African paths to development and engagement with the IPE. For example, in dealing the issue of poverty in South Africa, P. LenkaBula (2010) proposes to return to the basic concept of Ubuntu because it acknowledges the need for an improved quality of life among human beings. LenkaBula further develops the concept of Ubuntu or Botho, one of the viable principles for justice, which forces us to affirm those who are crushed by the economic structures of globalization. Her work emphasizes the essence of humanity, which is lived within the village or community. She associates the essential elements of Ubuntu with solidarity, cosmic relationality, and awareness of humanity's intimate connectedness with creation.

Furthermore, some of Nigeria's devout scholars of the political-economic Left—Jibril Ibrahim and Moses Ochonu, respectively—have come to see the virtues of Africapitalism for fostering Nigerian development (Ochuno 2015). Ibrahim applauds the efforts of Tony Elumelu for targeting production and youth development and entrepreneurship. Ochonu commends Africapitalism's challenge to craft a reasonable middle ground where capitalism is made to work for everyone, where everyone is a stakeholder, and where everyone partakes in the prosperity and value being created. Both agree that Africapitalism contains a set of operational values and ethics rooted in African culture that, if adopted by businesses and governmental actors, have the potential to create a new paradigm of shared economic development.

Cultural dimensions of political economy, including business culture, leadership subjectivity, and African identities in the analysis of the continent's progress in global development, reveal new and alternative African international political economies that are gradually emerging in localized African contexts. Whatever their variations, both Africapitalism and Ubuntu economics are rooted in the principles of self-determination, African agency, and African knowledge that reveal the Pan-Africanist, nationalist, and Africentric epistemologies of the new African business classes.

BIBLIOGRAPHY

Adi, Hakim. 2013. *Pan-Africanism and Communism: The Communist International, Africa and the Diaspora, 1919–1939.* Trenton, NJ: Africa World Press.

Africa Institute of South Africa. 2002. *Africa's Development Thinking since Independence: A Reader.* Pretoria: Africa Institute of South Africa.

Asabere-Ameyaw, Akwasi, J. Anamuah-Mensah, George J. Sefa Dei, and Kolawole Raheem. 2014. *Indigenist African Development and Related Issues: Towards a Transdisciplinary Perspective.* Rotterdam: Sense Publishers.

Balouga, Jean. 2012. "Nigerian Local Content: Challenges and Prospects." *International Association for Energy Economics,* Third Quarter: 23–26.

Best, Jacqueline, and Matthew Paterson. 2010. "Understanding Cultural Political Economy." In *Cultural Political Economy*, edited by J. Best and M. Paterson. RIPE Series. London: Routledge.

Chabal, Patrick. 2009. *Africa: The Politics of Suffering and Smiling*. London: Zed.

Cohen, D. L. and J. Daniel. 1981. *The Political Economy of Africa: Selected Readings*. London: Longman.

Dompere, K. K. 1992. *Africentricity and African Nationalism: Philosophy and Ideology for Africa's Complete Emancipation*. IAAS Pub.

Elumelu, Tony. 2014. WEF, Davos, January.

Escobar, Arturo. 1994. *Encountering Development: The Making and Unmaking of the Third World*. Princeton, NJ: Princeton University Press.

Green, R. H. and A.W Seidman. 1968. *Unity or Poverty: The Economics of Pan Africanism*. Baltimore, MD: Penguin Books.

Grosfoguel, Ramón. 2006. "Decolonizing Political-Economy and Post-Colonial Studies: Transmodernity, Border Thinking, and Global Coloniality." *Tabula Rasa* 4: 17–48.

Kebede, Messay. 1999. "Development and the African Philosophical Debate." *Journal of Sustainable Development in Africa* 1: Summer.

LenkaBula, P. 2010. "Economic Globalization, Ecumenical Theologies and Ethics of Justice in the Twenty-First Century." *Missionalia* 38: 99–120.

Lumumba-Kasongo, Tukumbi. 1994. *Political Re-Mapping of Africa: Transnational Ideology and the Re-Definition of Africa in World Politics*. Lanham, MD: University Press of America.

Maloka, Eddie. 2002. *Africa's Development Thinking since Independence: A Reader*. Pretoria Africa Institute of South Africa.

Marah, John. 1998. *African People in the Global Village: An Introduction to Pan African Studies* University Press of America.

Mignolo, Walter. 2000. *Local Histories/Global Designs: Coloniality, Subaltern Knowledges, and Border Thinking*. Princeton, NJ: Princeton University Press.

Mkandawire, Thandika. 2011. "Rethinking Africa's Re-Industrialisation and Regional Co-Operation: What Is the Best Way Forward?" In *Advocates for Change: How to Overcome Africa's Challenges*, edited by Moeletsi Mbeki. Johannesburg: Picador Africa.

Moyo, Ronald. 2015. "Ubuntu, Applying the African Cultural Concept to Business." *The African Exponent,* July 23.

Ndlovu-Gatsheni, Sabelo J. 2013. *Empire, Global Coloniality and African Subjectivity*. Berghahn Books.

Nsehe, Mfonobong. 2015. "1,000 African Entrepreneurs Selected by Tony Elumelu Foundation to Receive Grant & Training." *Africa Events,* Accessed March 8, 2016.

Ochonu, Moses. 2015. *Premium Times,* August 27.

Opoku, Agyeman. 2004. *The Failure of Grassroots Pan-Africanism: The Case of the All-African Trade Union Federation*. Lexington Books.

Appendix A

Descriptions of Variables
Used in Analyses

SOCIAL GROUPS

1. African Americans—Respondent identified race as African American.
2. Caribbeans—Respondent identified race as African American.

DEPENDENT VARIABLE

Affirmative Action—"Affirmative action refers to any policy or law used to give qualified individuals equal access to employment, education, business, and contracting opportunities. Generally speaking, do you think affirmative action is a good thing or a bad thing?" -1 = "a bad thing," 0 = "neither good nor bad," 1 = "a good thing."

INDEPENDENT VARIABLES

1. Hardworking—"Imagine a seven-point scale on which the characteristics of the people in a group can be rated. In the first question a score of 1 means you think almost all of the people in that group tend to be 'lazy.' A score of 7 means that you think that most people in the group are 'hardworking.' A score of 4 means that you think most people in the group are not closer to one end or the other, and of course, you may choose any number in between." *Hardworking African Americans:* the score assigned African Americans. *Hardworking Caribbeans:* the score assigned Caribbeans.
2. Discrimination—"Now I would like to ask you about how much discrimination or unfair treatment you think different groups face in the U.S.

151

Do you think the following groups face a lot of discrimination, some, a little, or no discrimination at all?" *Discrimination African American*: "How about African Americans?" *Discrimination Caribbeans*: "How about Caribbeans?" 1 = none, 2 = a little, 3 = some, 4 = a lot.

Racial Resentment

1. Minorities Blame—"If racial and ethnic minorities don't do well in life they have no one to blame but themselves." 1= strongly disagree, 2 = somewhat disagree, 3 = somewhat agree, 4 = strongly agree.
2. Bootstraps—"Irish, Italians, Jewish, and many other minorities overcame prejudice and worked their way up. Blacks should do the same without any special favors." 1= strongly disagree, 2 = somewhat disagree, 3 = somewhat agree, 4 = strongly agree.
3. Blacks Deserve—"Over the past few years, Blacks have gotten less than they deserve." 1= strongly disagree, 2 = somewhat disagree, 3 = somewhat agree, 4 = strongly agree.

CONTROL VARIABLES

1. Age—Respondent's age in years, ranging from 17 to 100.
2. Gender—1 = male, 0 = female.
3. Education—Highest grade or level of school respondent completed. 1= less than high school, 2 = high school diploma, 3 = some college, 4 = college graduate, 5 = graduate school.
4. Family Income—Dollar amount of respondent and respondent's family's total income from all sources.
5. South—Respondent lives in the South (AL, AR, DE, DC, FL, GA, KY, LA, MD, MS, NC, OK, SC, TN, TX, VA, WV).
6. Liberal—"We hear a lot of talk these days about liberals and conservatives. When it comes to politics, do you usually think of yourself as liberal or conservative?" 1 = liberal, 0 otherwise.
7. Conservative—"We hear a lot of talk these days about liberals and conservatives. When it comes to politics, do you usually think of yourself as liberal or conservative?" 1 = conservative, 0 otherwise.
8. Democrat—"Generally speaking, do you usually think of yourself as a Republican, a Democrat, an Independent, or something else?" 1 = Democrat, 0 otherwise.
9. Republican—"Generally speaking, do you usually think of yourself as a Republican, a Democrat, an Independent, or something else?" 1 = Republican, 0 otherwise.

10. Ideology—1= Extremely Conservative, 2 = Conservative, 3 = Slightly Conservative, 4 = Moderate or Middle of the Road, 5 = Slightly Liberal, 6 = Liberal, 7 = Extremely Liberal.
11. Party Identification—"Generally speaking, do you usually think of yourself as a..." -1 = Republican, 0 = Independent or Other or No Preference, 1 = Democrat.

Index

Page references with figures and tables are italicized.

Shabazz, Ishmail (UBAD co-founder), 66–67
Shaft (film), 125
Shapiro, Thomas, 124
Shelton, Jason E., 103–19, 105, 108
Shihadeh, Edward, 82
Shipler, David (*The Working Poor*), 96
Shoeman, Assad, 62, 63
Sidanius, Jim, 45
Sigelman, Lee, 105, 107
Slap Shot (film), 39
Slatton, Brittany, 21–34
Smith, Christian, 105
Smith, Eliot R., 105
Smith, Jacob, 23
Sniderman, Paul, 108
Soberanis, Antonio (labor organizer), 62, 63, 68
social stratification:
 benefits, for low income workers, 80;
 Civil Rights movement, 79, 80;
 competition, for economic resources *vs.* social space, 76–77;
 crime reduction and, 82–83;
 definition, 9–10;
 economies of scale, 77;
 future research issues, 83;
 of immigrants, 81;
 by mass incarceration of Blacks, 81–82;
 politics/voting and, 76–77;
 prison labor and, 81–82;
 "racial stratification," 79–80;
 residential segregation, 80–81;
 school desegregation, 77;
 social space and income, of African Americans, 106–7;
 "spatial mismatch," 81;
 suburban neighborhoods, 77;
 voting effectiveness, 76;
 workplace and, 78–79.
 See also stratification economics
South Africa. *See* Ubuntu economic philosophy, in South Africa
Spelman, William, 82
Staine, Calvert (Belize UNIA), 62

Sterling, Donald (ex-owner, Los Angeles Clippers), 21
Stewart, James, 71–85, 75
Stoll, Michael, 81
stratification economics, 13–18, 71–83;
 collective racial identity, commodities *vs.* direct contact, 75–76;
 collective racial identity *vs.* "public goods," 74;
 competition, discrimination and, 73;
 definition, 15;
 "economic coercion," 76;
 "economics of discrimination," 72–73;
 groups, economic competition among, 74–75;
 groups, importance of, 71, 73–74;
 "human homogeneity postulate," 13, 14–15;
 intergroup competition, 76;
 neoclassical economics, 72–73;
 race, in neoclassical economics, 72;
 race and racial identity, 71–72;
 racial discrimination and, 17;
 as theory on race and inequality, 14;
 "whiteness," disparities in social conditions and, 16–17
Stuart, Merah S. (*An Economic Detour*), 126–27
Student Nonviolent Coordinating Committee (SNCC), 91
Sweet Sweetback's Badass Song (film), 125

Taft-Hartley Act of 1947, 91
Tarman, Christopher, 23
Tate, Katherine, 108
Tellinger, Michael (entrepreneur), 147
Tembo, C., 43
Temple, Edward, 47
Thomas, A. J., 46
Thompson, A., 40–41
Thorton, Michael C., 107
Till, Emmitt, financial support for family of, 93

About the Editor and Contributors

EDITOR

James L. Conyers, Jr., is director of the African American Studies Program, director of the Center for African American Culture, and University Professor of African American Studies at the University of Houston. He is the author or editor of thirty-five books and currently serves on the editorial board of the *Journal of Black Studies*. Additionally, Dr. Conyers serves as an external referee to the *Journal of the American Academy of Religion*, and the *Ethnic Studies Review*. He is the founding editor of the serial, *Africana Studies: A Review of Social Science Research* and series editor of Africana Studies at Transaction Publishers. His current publication is an edited volume titled, *Africana Islamic Studies*. Additionally, he is at work on an intellectual biography of the late Charles H. Wesley. His educational background includes BA in Communications from Ramapo College of New Jersey (1983), MA in Africana Studies from the State University of New York at Albany (1984), PhD in African American Studies from Temple University (1992), and graduate training in Oral History at Columbia University (1995). He was married to Jacqueline I. Conyers (25 years, who passed in 2006) and has three sons, Chad Hawkins (29 years), Sekou Conyers (25 years)—a professional athlete, former student athlete, and alumni of Texas A&M University at Commerce and Northeastern Oklahoma A&M College, is currently a certified PE teacher in the Pasadena Independent School District—and Kamau Conyers (22 years), a senior student athlete at Prairie View A&M University and graduate of Blinn College, in Brenham, Texas.

CONTRIBUTORS

Drew Brown, PhD, is an assistant professor of Africana Studies at the University of Delaware. His most recent publication is "The Portrayal of Black Masculinity in the NFL: Critical Race Theory and the Images of Black Males" in *Critical Race Theory and American Sport*, Billy Hawkins, Carter-Francique, and Cooper (New York: Palgrave Macmillan), pp. 217–246, 2016.

Latasha Chaffin, PhD, is an assistant professor in the Political Science Department at the College of Charleston. Her most recent publication is a coauthored article with Christopher A. Cooper and H. Gibbs Knotts (December 2017) titled "Furling the Flag: Explaining the 2015 Vote to Remove the Confederate Flag in South Carolina." *Politics & Policy*. 45 (6), 1–20.

James L. Conyers, Jr., PhD, is director of the African American Studies Program and Director of the Center for the Study of African American Culture, and university professor of African American Studies at the University of Houston. He is the editor or author of over thirty-five books. His most recent publication is *Molefi Kete Asante: A Critical Afrocentric Reader*, Peter Lang Publishers (2017).

Rita Kiki Edozie, PhD, is professor of Global and African Affairs and Associate Dean at the McCormack Graduate School of Policy and Global Studies at the University of Massachusetts-Boston. She has written six books, including her latest book *Pan Africa Rising: The Cultural Political Economy of Nigeria's Afri-Capitalism and South Africa's Ubuntu Business* (Palgrave-MacMillan, 2017).

Anthony D. Greene, PhD, is an assistant professor of African American Studies and Sociology in the Department of Sociology & Anthropology at the College of Charleston. He is the coauthor with Jason E. Shelton of the article titled "No Fault of Their Own? Beliefs about the Causes of Racial Inequality among American Blacks, West Indian and African Immigrants." Forthcoming (Fall 2017). *Issues in Race & Society: An Interdisciplinary Global Journal*.

Devon Lee, is currently working as an Adjunct Professor at Radford University. He is a doctoral candidate in the Department of Sociology at Virginia Tech University.

Maurice Mangum, PhD, is Chair and associate professor in the Department of Political Science and Criminal Justice at North Carolina A&T State

University. His forthcoming publication is entitled *Assimilation and Black Immigrants: Comparing the Racial Identity and Racial Consciousness of Caribbeans and African Americans. National Political Science Review National Political Science Review,* coauthored with Anthony Rodriguez.

Gregory Price, PhD, is professor of economics at Morehouse. His previous appointments include interim dean, School of Business, Langston University; Charles E. Merrill Professor and Chair, Department of Economics, Morehouse College; Director of the Mississippi Urban Research Center; Professor of Economics at Jackson State University; and economics program director at the National Science Foundation. He also served as president of the National Economic Association in 2008. An applied econometrician and theorist, his current research interests include economic anthropometry, the economics of historically Black colleges/universities, the effects of race on economic stratification, and the causes/consequences of slavery. His most recent publication *Climate Change and Cross-National Islamist Terrorism in Nigeria, in Peace Economics, Peace Science, and Public Policy* (2017), provides evidence that climate change is a potential driver of Islamist terrorism in Sub-Saharan Africa. A native of New Haven, Connecticut, Dr. Price earned his BA in economics from Morehouse College, and completed his economics doctorate at the University of Wisconsin–Milwaukee.

Brittany Slatton, PhD, is an associate professor of Sociology at Texas Southern University. Her most recent publication is an article titled "I've Got My Family and My Faith: Black Women and the Suicide Paradox." *Socius: Sociological Research for a Dynamic World,* coauthored with Kamesha Spates.

Jason E. Shelton, PhD, is the director of the Center for African American Studies and associate professor of sociology, at University of Texas-Arlington. His forthcoming publication is an article titled "Black Reltrad: The Measure for Testing Religious Diversity and Commonality among African Americans." *Journal for the Scientific Study of Religion*, coauthored with Ryon J. Cobb.

Marcia Walker-McWilliams is an associate director in the Center for Civic Leadership at Rice University. She received her doctorate in American history from the University of Chicago. She is the author of *Reverend Addie Wyatt: Faith and the Fight for Labor, Gender and Racial Equality* (Urbana: University of Illinois Press, 2016).

Robert E. Weems, Jr., PhD, is the Willard W. Garvey Distinguished Professor of Business History at Wichita State University. His most recent publication is the coedited book (with Jason P. Chambers), *Building The Black Metropolis: African American Entrepreneurship in Chicago* published by the University of Illinois Press (2017).

www.ingramcontent.com/pod-product-compliance
Lightning Source LLC
Chambersburg PA
CBHW021818270326
41932CB00007B/235